THE WORK
OF THE
PASTOR

D0928733

THE WORK OF THE PASTOR

William Still

Published by Rutherford House

and Christian Focus Publications

First published 1984

This edition published 2001
by Rutherford House, 17 Claremont Park, Edinburgh
EH6 7PJ, Scotland, and Christian Focus Publications,
Geanies House, Fearn, Ross-shire, IV20 1TW, Scotland

06 05 04 03 02 01   8 7 6 5 4 3

British Library Cataloguing in Publication Data

ISBN 0-946068-63-1

Typeset by Rutherford House, Edinburgh
and printed by
T.J. International Ltd., Padstow, Cornwall

CONTENTS

AUTHOR'S PREFACE

These five addresses were given, two at the Inter-Varsity Theological Students' Conference at Swanwick, December, 1964, and three, a sequel to the two, at the Inter-Varsity Theological Students' Conference in Northern Ireland, December, 1965; the latter under the title, *The Ministry in 1966.*

The connection between the two sets of addresses is that some Irish theological students at the Swanwick Conference of 1964 invited the speaker to come to Larne the following year and repeat these addresses; but the title subsequently given called for new material.

Some may think the Irish addresses scarcely deal with the pastoral side of the ministry, but it depends on what is meant by the pastoral ministry. The thesis is that the pastor, being the shepherd of the flock, feeds the flock upon God's Word; the bulk of pastoral work is therefore through the ministry of the Word. Only the residue of problems and difficulties remaining require to be dealt with thereafter.

These five addresses on the work of the pastor have been around for a long time. The book of them has gone through several editions and has been reproduced in different publications, and I believe it is still valued. I knew when these addresses were given me by the Spirit that they contained some of the best insights the Lord has afforded me, and I am glad that their message is abidingly relevant to the greatest work ever given to man, the work of the pastor.

William Still, Aberdeen

Chapter One

'FEED MY SHEEP'

The Pastor

Before we look at the work of the pastor we must look at the pastor himself. The pastor by definition is a shepherd, the under-shepherd of the flock of God. His primary task is to feed the flock by leading them to green pastures. He also has to care for them when they are sick or hurt, and seek them when they go astray. The importance of the pastor depends on the value of the sheep.

Pursue the pastoral metaphor a little further: Israel's sheep were reared, fed, tended, retrieved, healed and restored—for sacrifice on the altar of God. This end of all pastoral work must never be forgotten—that its ultimate aim is to lead God's people to offer themselves up to Him in total devotion of worship and service.

Many who are called pastors, having lost the end in view, or never having seen it, become pedlars of various sorts of wares, gulling the people and leading them into their own power. And when they fail to gather a clientele for their own brand of merchandise they uptail and away, for they are not really interested in the flock of God; they were using them only as a means of their own aggrandisement, to boost their ego and indulge their desire for power. 'The hireling fleeth, because he is an hireling [he is in it for what he can get out of it], and careth not for the sheep' (John 10:13). Whereas the Good Shepherd careth for the sheep—even unto death; and, therefore, seeks so to care for them that He may at last present them without blemish unto God.

But there are different kinds of flocks, goats as well as sheep. A pastor may find himself in the midst of a generally nominal church membership. How is he going to turn a flock of goats into a flock of sheep? For sheep they must become. To quote James Packer:

> The assumption implied and often implicit in Calvin's handling of the theme of the Christian life, is that only Christians are in a position to live it. The Christian life is for Christian men only. The

point looks obvious as soon as it is stated, but, nevertheless, we need to dwell on it, not only because it is fundamental to everything that follows, but also because it would be rash to assume without discussion that twentieth century churchmen (and chapel men!) are of Calvin's mind as to what a Christian is. To Calvin the Christian is utterly different from other men.

And if I may add to Dr Packer's quotation, Christian men are different from other men, particularly in believing that there is an alternative destiny for men. So that the pastor called to feed the sheep may find that his first calling is to evangelise the goats!

The Pastor as Evangelist

Evangelists are a separate gift to the church from pastors and teachers (one office in Eph. 4:11), set between apostles and prophets on the one hand, and pastors and teachers on the other. Evangelists are not mentioned at all in the list of ministries in 1 Corinthians 12:1–18. But the pastor must be an evangelist all the time—all are evangelists in the primary sense of showing forth Christ (Matt. 5:16); and as soon as he has a handful of converted members, even one, on his hands, he must at once shepherd, that is, feed them. And you don't feed sheep on mere Gospel addresses. Paul's charge to young Timothy is to,

> Preach the word, be instant in season and out of season; convince, rebuke, exhort with all long suffering and teaching. For the time will come when they will not endure sound teaching, but their ears will itch for tales and fables and they will refuse the truth. But watch thou in all things, endure afflictions, do the work of an evangelist, make full proof of thy ministry (2 Tim. 4:2–5).

This is the work of pastor, teacher and evangelist, combined.

In a Bible Study on the subject of evangelism and teaching in Paul's ministry, John Duncan (Professor of Mathematics) alleged:

> There is no clear distinction in the Acts between what may be called Paul's 'evangelistic ministry' and his 'teaching ministry'. In both, we find him expounding the Scriptures (and writing new Scriptures!). When his hearers were mainly unconverted we might call the ministry evangelistic or kerugmatic (*e.g.* at Lystra, Athens, and at Cornelius' home); and when mainly Christian, we might call the ministry teaching or didactic. But there is a wide range between these situations, and

some of Paul's evangelism involves major pieces of Old Testament exposition.

Dodd, I think, holds that the distinction between *kerygma* and *didache* in the Acts is clear cut. 'Too clear cut', says F. F. Bruce. 'For several purposes,' he says, 'it is a convenient distinction, but in the New Testament there is a considerable overlap between the two.'

James Philip of Holyrood Abbey, Edinburgh, taking up the question of the relation between *kerygma* and *didache* (preaching and teaching) and noting that Locke in the International Critical Commentary renders 2 Timothy 4:5, 'Do the work of one who has a Gospel to preach', maintains that the emphasis is upon *euangelion* (the Gospel) rather than on *euangelistes* (the evangelist). He goes on:

> Whether this be a true interpretation or not, it does serve to underline the fact that it is misleading to identify 'preaching the Gospel' with 'preaching an evangelistic message'. All the evidence of the New Testament goes to show that the apostles' evangelism was a teaching evangelism. All the characteristic messages in Acts have the kerygma at their heart; but it was doctrinal preaching all the time, based on the Scriptures, expounding and

interpreting them. 'Paul, as his manner was...reasoned (or argued) with them out of the scriptures, opening and alleging...' (Acts 17:2, 3). Rightly understood, apostolic evangelism is not a matter of exhorting and pressing men to come to Christ until there has been a proclamation of the mighty acts of God in Christ in reconciliation and redemption, and on the basis of this, the free offer of His grace is made to all who will receive it.

It follows, therefore, that the church's evangelism ought to be one in which all the counsel of God is made known to men. We need a recovery of belief in the converting and sanctifying power of the living Word of God in the teaching of the pulpit, and its ability to transform the lives of men and produce in them the lineaments and fruits of mature Christian character.

Teacher and Preacher

All this suggests that if a man declares the whole counsel of the Word of God contained in the Bible, then he must be both teaching and preaching. I suggest to you that such a thorough, radical ministry is so little known today that most people, even in the evangelical church, have not the faintest idea of its effects and fruits. For where this total ministry is energised by the prayers of saints who mean business with God, the effect upon the unconverted person happening into the midst of such a fellowship will be as Paul describes when he says,

> He will be convinced [convicted] of all, judged, examined, searched, sifted by all; and thus the secrets of his heart are made manifest; and so falling down on his face he will worship God, and report that God is among you of a truth (1 Cor. 14:24, 25).

Of course, the sense of the presence of God, and the cutting edge of His Word, may make him mad, so that he rushes out, bangs the door, and goes and reports you to the authorities… He may come back! This is equally to be expected where the power of the mighty God is unleashed. You cannot expect to have the one without the other. But too many today pin their faith for fruitful evangelism on harping for ever on a few Gospel facts isolated from the broad and full context of the whole Bible.

We were thinking about this in our fellowship in a discussion of a programme 'Instant Salvation', broadcast by the BBC's Radio 3, when our lawyer elder, Francis Lyall, who had spent a year in Canada and the United States, pointed out that Gospel facts are poured over the air twenty-four hours a Sunday across the water, and few there can really claim to be ignorant of them. 'But,' he said, 'there seemed to me to be little evidence that the dispelling of ignorance on that level had much effect in increasing the vital Christian constituency.' We have had in our congregation the curious experience of a number of academic evangelicals of different denominations coming to church and complaining that they could not take their unconverted friends to a ministry of continual systematic teaching of the Word. Why not? Some of the most thoroughly converted people I know were converted through a teaching ministry. One of them, converted in our church hall, became President of the Cambridge Inter-Collegiate Christian Union.

Feed the Sheep!

Certainly, we must not make the disastrous error of going on preaching what is called the simple Gospel, isolating a few mere facts, wonderful as they are, until the last man-jack is known to have been converted. What are all the hungry sheep going to do until then? Jesus will tell you what to do with them—not in word, but in deed. When the Galileans made it clear that they wanted the fruits of Christ's kingdom in healing to their bodies, but not His teaching about the nature of the kingdom, He turned and ran from them up a mountain, to teach (feed) His disciples. For our Lord came to do three things, in an ascending scale of importance: to show forth the powers of His kingdom in healing the sick; to teach the tiny nucleus who would listen to Him and who were to be the hope of the church after His ascension; and—His greatest reason for coming—to die. Next to that (His death and rising, which gave sanction and power to all the rest) He must needs teach a nucleus the laws of His kingdom; so He gave them the Sermon on the Mount. Such teaching is essential food for sheep.

It is to feed sheep on such truth that men are called to churches and congregations, whatever they may think they are called to do. If you think that you are called to keep a largely worldly organisation, miscalled a church, going, with infinitesimal doses of innocuous sub-Christian drugs or stimulants, then the only help I can give you is to advise you to give up the hope of the ministry and go and be a street scavenger; a far healthier and more godly job, keeping the streets tidy, than cluttering the church with a lot of worldly claptrap in the delusion that you are doing a job for God. The pastor is called to feed the sheep, even if the sheep do not want to be fed. He is certainly not to become an entertainer of goats. Let goats entertain goats, and let them do it out in goatland. You will certainly not turn goats into sheep by pandering to their goatishness. Do we really believe that the Word of God, by His Spirit, changes, as well as maddens men? If we do, to be evangelists and pastors, feeders of sheep, we must be men of the Word of God.

The Word of God

Now, consider what this means: the Word of God, the law of God, 'the royal law according to the scriptures', 'the perfect law of liberty', is a sort of rational, verbal, imprint, transcript expression, or descriptive mould of the character of God, which character became incarnate and human in Jesus Christ. 'He is,' says the writer to the Hebrews, 'the character, the express image [the matrix, stamp, engraving] of the Person or substance of God' (Heb. 1:3). But this written Word, summed up in the incarnate Word, not only expresses what God is like, but is and becomes by the operation of the Spirit of God, the nourishment by which we become like Him also. To be a pastor of the sheep, a feeder of the Word to others, you must be fed yourself.

No man can make the Bible become the Word of God for today (I know that it is, I am not selling you Barth at his worst!) to feed the flock of God by simply 'passing on' what it says. Food has to be assimilated and absorbed by digestion. An atheist could 'teach' the Bible, and some try to in our schools! That will not do. The Word became flesh, and it must become flesh again in you. It is godly character which is the real pastor, or is the basis of him. You have heard the saying that a man's words could not be heard because what he was and did spoke so loudly. Well, it takes the whole Word of God, impartially received but rightly divided, to make a rounded, full-orbed character, which every pastor, within his God-given limitations, must be. 'Brethren,' says the Apostle, 'be not adolescents in understanding [in your minds]: howbeit, in malice be infants [harmless as doves; having no part with evil, so that, standing back from it, you may see it as it is, in contrast to its opposite], but in understanding, be full-grown [*teleioi*, mature, manly]' (1 Cor. 14:20). To be true pastors, your whole life must be spent in knowing the truth of this Word, not only verbally, propositionally, theologically, but religiously, that is, devotionally, morally, in worshipping Him whom it reveals, and in personal obedience to Him whose commands it contains, in all the promised grace and threat of those commands. To be pastors you must be 'fed men', not only in knowledge, but in wisdom, grace, humility, courage, fear of God, and fearlessness of men.

A Poor Diet

Courage is the greatest lack today. If all men in the ministry acted upon what they know we would have a far better ministry. Yet, the ignorance is colossal. Your ignorance of the Word may be colossal. And what can we do to help that in one sermon? I have little hope of any one learning categorically, decisively, from me unless he or she is prepared to sit consistently, almost exclusively, for years under the ministry of the Word of God: thereafter, he or she will spend their whole life digesting it. This is what I wrote recently about spiritual 'vagrants' amongst the students who drop into our church:

I despair of some who come to our church and who read our literature, because what they hear and read is only one item of their spiritual diet. Indeed, they eat very little of anything but like children play with their food. That is why they are so thin. They juggle with it as if it were something to sell, not eat, and are not very sure which item is the best selling line.

The advice to them was:

Eat it, eat it whole. All or nothing. For it is only 'all or nothing' devourers of the Word of God who will ever be or do anything for God.

Extreme? Yes; but there is no other way of knowing for sure that this is the way of ways than by swallowing the message whole. And that is not an experiment; it is a committal. But obedience to the truth demands nothing less. Knowledge without obedience is useless. You must be doers as well as hearers of the Word in your own lives. This alone will make the image of Jesus Christ appear in your life so that you exemplify your teaching in your own person before you begin to teach. Then your hearers will receive both the teacher and his teaching.

Spirit-Inspired

There is, of course, only one Teacher, the Holy Spirit (*cf.* John 14:16, 17, 26; 16:7–15). And if the Holy Spirit is not in our hearts, in our life and in all our teaching of the Word of God (and He will not be if our characters are not being moulded according to the moral and spiritual pattern of the Word), then we had better not open our mouths. For there is nothing so boring, stale, flat and unprofitable as holy things retailed in the absence of the Spirit. This is one of the devil's most cunning tricks, to cause the Word of God to be dispensed by lazy, sleepy, moribund creatures, who find preaching the most burdensome part of their work and cannot help showing it. I have heard people praying, preaching and teaching, and have been so desolated and my heart has been so opposed to the whole depressing exercise, that I have almost wished the things they said were not true so that I could refute them. The whole soul of man, even ungodly man, cries out against the Word of God as a dead thing. Where the Spirit of God is, there may and will be unpleasant manifestations, but there will not be boredom. Division there will be, some for and some against—that is another story—but there will be life, and the Word of God will cut and melt ice, even if it confirms the unmeltability of some ice, which is even hardened by the Word of God. Change the metaphor to steel, and you will understand what I am trying to say.

Things will happen. The preaching of the Word of God, when it flows through a living vessel dedicated utterly to the Master's use, is not only an event in the lives of those who hear it but becomes, first a decisive act, and then, necessary food for their souls. My whole concern in my work of trying to make pastors (and I have 'made' too few, although I have had many men through my hands) is that they become men of God; then, the pastoral work will look after itself. It will still have to be done. But the man of God is made for that.

The question is: Are you on the way to becoming men of God? I am not really concerned with anything else until men are. I am sure that some of you are. None of us has arrived! Do you, then, know the Spirit of God teaching you the Word, in private, and in the fellowship of the saints? We learn in fellowship. This may have nothing to do with lectures, although it should have everything to do with them if your lecturers are men of God. Unless the Word of God works for you, and solves the problems of your own life (I do not mean perfectly, but in the sense that you know where you are in relation to them), how can you expect that you will be able to make it work for others? One of the great sorrows of my life is that men who have gone through my hands are out in the ministry and, because of what seems to be disobedience to the Word, or it may be because they were never called to it at all, they have not yet begun to solve their own problems. The Word has not had a chance to do its own work in them. What can they do for others? Nothing!

Be Sure of Your Calling

Then, when you are sure that God has laid his hand upon you to be His child and servant as pastor and teacher of the Word of God—I wonder what proportion of you will yet find out that you were never called by God to do this and will therefore be spewed out of the ministry by the Spirit of God in the next few years to become something else, deputation secretaries, *etc.* (this is not to despise deputation secretaries, for not all deputation secretaries are rejects from the ministry; some had the courage and humility in the first place to know their God-given calling, not being carnally ambitious)—when you are sure of your calling as pastors and teachers, then you must be wholly geared to that life. This involves first, the building up of your own faith by feeding on the Word of God; then obeying it; so that you may make your sole task in life to teach the whole Word of God to your flock. The whole Word: this is pastoral work. Take Paul's example in Ephesus (Acts 20:24–32). We are not called to make a crowd of worldly folk happy—even worldly evangelistic folk happy—but so to labour amongst them that, through many tribulations, discouragements and misunderstandings, we form a faithful people of God, however small a remnant of the total congregation that may be. There will be many opposers, some very surprising ones! I could bring ministers of various denominations to testify that although the unconverted in their congregations made their lives miserable, the most fiendish persecutions have come from evangelistic people who wanted a perpetual preaching of that part of the Gospel which they thought (often wrongly) did not touch them, and who, when the Word of God in its fullness was unleashed upon them, went virtually mad with rage. There is nothing too vile for such people to do when their futile evangelistic round with its patronage of the unconverted has been ended, and the myth of their conceited superiority has been destroyed. It takes a courageous man in these circumstances to preach the whole Word of God without fear or favour, whoever it hurts—himself, his loved ones, his friends, or his enemies.

Preach the <u>Whole</u> Word

Having seen that a pastor is called to live by the whole Word of God in order that he may teach the whole Word of God, how is he to begin? There are, generally, three methods that I know of.

Firstly, he can follow the church Year and broadly cover the substance of the Word of God annually. He can preach through the Bible, book by book, alternating Old and New Testaments, and different parts of each judiciously, to give a balanced diet. This demands continual specific guidance of the Holy Spirit. Each situation is unique and only God Himself can tell a man the order in which to take the books. Do you think you would know divine guidance here?

Secondly, the pastor can teach the Word of God, subject by subject. This may be done evangelistically where there is not much of a clue as to the fundamentals of the Gospel, just as he may turn to more 'edifying' subjects amongst a congregation thoroughly grounded on the Word.

Thirdly, the pastor can preach his way through one of the creeds, or through the chapters of the Westminster Confession of Faith, or the Thirty-Nine Articles.

But, remember, it is not syntheses of the Word of God, not doctrinal presentations of the Word, but the very Word of God itself, read, commented upon, expounded, and its parts vitally and intelligently related, that does the work in men's hearts. For example, for fifty years, in one place, I have preached through the Bible, book by book, chapter by chapter, verse by verse, New Testament and Old Testament several times. I have written Daily Bible Reading Notes continually since 1947, and have commented on the whole Bible several times. Now, the principal product of this is not a mass of sermon notes, statistics or a pile of booklets containing at least two commentaries on the whole Bible. The product is the lives that are loving and serving

Christ in various parts of the world, not least in the ministry in its various denominations.

Nobody is going to exclaim over my sermon notes, or prize my Bible Reading Notes as literary or scholarly gems—although people who have despised them have had to change their minds when, in some personal need, they have found in them correction for their lives and food and comfort for their souls. I hate writing this and laying myself open to possible misunderstanding, but even in the ministry the criteria of pastoral work may be mistaken. Indeed, the criteria by which you judge what you are reading now may be seriously mistaken, and you may be wondering when I am going to get down to my subject. But this is my subject: first, feeding the flock of God, then, tending them in their need. All this, the healing as well as the feeding, flows from the ministry of the Word of God in the power of the Spirit. If only I could make you believe that!

Side Effects!

My pastoral work of personal dealing, considerable though it is, has been greatly reduced through the years because the building up of people's faith, by the ministry of the Word of God, solves so much in their lives. It enables those who receive it and seek to live by it to understand and solve so much in other lives, that instead of becoming a liability on my time and energy, they become pastors themselves. Indeed, one of the features of such a radical and total ministry of the Word is that it thrusts so many into spiritual and social work that I can hardly keep a congregation together on account of their scattering throughout the land, and indeed, the earth.

I don't know about other countries, but in Scotland the great emphasis today is on the witness of the layman. Quite right! It should be. And there is only one way to make Christian laymen rise to their responsibilities fruitfully, and that is to turn them into thoroughly Christian characters. You will then find that even in a comparatively small fellowship there will emerge a surprising range and variety of working gifts of the Spirit.

From time to time I am tempted to try and count how many of our folk are engaged in medical, nursing, and psychiatric work; social welfare work amongst babies, children, delinquents and maladjusted adolescents; in geriatrics, health visiting, serving as Christians in

Law, Civil Service, teaching, lecturing, *etc.*; applying their skills as Christians in the world with a witness to give and a task to do. But there are so many that I cannot count them, and I am not going to. The true statistics are kept 'upstairs', where the computers and computors are quite accurate, even though they do not publish their figures down here.

The Basics of Effective Ministry

Now, what are the basics of a ministry which transforms the character of all sorts of people? First, the pastor must know Christ, really know Him, and live his life as sifted by His all-searching holiness all the time. This is the only way to produce any fruit, to say nothing of any satisfaction, nor indeed any fun in his life.

Second (and it does not follow that all such thoroughly Christian characters will be called to the ministry of the Word), you must know that God has called you with a heavenly compulsion, whether you want it or not, to be an evangelist, pastor and teacher of His Word.

Third, you must find out His will for your life, and His place for you, and obey the fiery cloud, as Israel did in the wilderness, as your only safety and satisfaction, whatever your inclinations are, or what your loved ones, sweethearts, friends, or even your enemies say. You must remember, of course, that God is the most sweetly reasonable and considerate Person in the world when we give Him His place. But also remember that He is ruthless to the disobedient.

Fourth, having been called or appointed to minister to a local congregation, begin to minister the Word of God to them at once, depending for all you are worth on the Holy Spirit, and believing that this is the biggest thing you can do for them in all the world. This is your life: not a part of it, but your life. Other things come in, of course, but this is your life, the most thrilling life any one can live on earth, to expose a group of people, Christian or not, to the all-searching eye of the Word of God. Do you remember what the writer to the Hebrews says about it?

> For the Word of God is quick [living] and powerful [efficient, *energes*], and sharper than any two-edged sword, even penetrating to the division of both soul and spirit, of joints and marrow, and is a discerner of the thoughts and intents of the heart. And there is not a created thing unapparent before Him, but all things are naked and laid bare to the eyes of Him with whom is our account (Heb. 4:12, 13).

Prayer

As you begin, let the people know that your ministry of the Word is going to be soaked in prayer; your own, and that of those who will join you. Set a time for prayer, but do not say there will be prayer if any one comes, but rather that you will be there to pray at such-and-such an hour and that you will be glad to join with any who come. The fact that you mean business will be the surest indication to your people that God means business with them. If this continues and grows, as it must if God be with you, then a power-house will be created which will determine your ministry. This outpouring of prayer will guide you in your choices and sequences of teaching, and provide impetus, thrust, drive and power. It will produce in you that compassion and tenderness that will mark your ministry as of God, along with that authority and sternness which will cause the people to know that God is in the midst of the work.

Early Fruits

He will work, slowly as it may seem at first. Your quiet persistence—this charge, or parish, or living is not a mere stepping-stone to a better appointment: God has caused you to become pastor to some souls here who are as valuable to Him as any in the world—your quiet persistence will be a sign that you believe God has a purpose of grace for this people, and that this purpose of grace will be promoted, not by gimmicks, or stunts, or new ideas, but by the Word of God released in preaching by prayer.

There will soon be evidence that God is at work—and the devil will rouse himself too! The first sign may be that believing folk who may have grown cold and worldly, will begin to loosen their purse-strings out of thankfulness to God for His living Word, and the finances will improve. This is the least of the signs, but it is almost always the first to appear in the reviving of a church.

Then this becomes a witness to the nominal in the midst, the materially minded, that a faithful ministry pays financial as well as spiritual dividends. There will be opposition, and you may be quite surprised at where it comes from—notably those who have been 'running the church' and who have turned the church of Jesus Christ into their private preserve and hobby. Those whose daily lives do not match up to their profession will begin to be disturbed. Those who maintain class distinctions, social or intellectual, in the congregation, and all who put up with the fulminations of a young minister as long as he does not seriously interfere with their *status quo*, will begin to panic. Amidst all this, consciences will be stirred and lives will be searched, home life, business, church activities examined. People will begin to take sides, objections to you and to what you preach, and how you preach it, will become increasingly plausible (but quite irrational when you consider them). Your manner, length and style of preaching, *etc.* will all be torn to pieces.

Withal, there will appear a nucleus of responsive souls all very imperfect; some perhaps quite objectionable, and possibly, alas, without a good witness in the church and community; some toadying to the new man and to the new-found livingness of his message in the hope that, siding with you, they may escape the searchingness of the Word, and put themselves in your good books. But a nucleus will appear, of whom several will be seen to be truly devoted to God, and bound together by ties of holy love. These will honour you for your faithfulness to God. God will even provide you with a suitable comforter, someone to care for you in the upheaval, and you will begin to see the church taking apostolic shape before your eyes. You will see the Word changing and exposing lives, and you will marvel and tremble and rejoice and fear all in one. You will be bowed in profoundest humility before God when you see that He has called you to follow in the train, however far behind, of the first apostles, and the prophets, teachers and martyrs of the centuries.

In this work we must not be afraid of upset. We must not go out of our way to create it; we don't look for trouble, but seek peace. But if we are going to be faithful to God and to men, there will be upset. The great thing to know is that God is at work creatively, through His Word, in answer to the prayers of His people. There is not a greater task a man can perform in the whole world than this, that he is being used to release the all-searching Word of God upon a company of needy souls. It is the most amazing thing. It works! God works. His Word works. Prayer works. The Spirit works.

Failure to Feed the Flock

Do you still think I am merely skirting the fringe of my subject? I can hardly hope to give you more than an introduction to it. If I can expose to you some of the multifarious reasons why the Lord's called servants do *not* become true and faithful pastors and teachers of the Word and feeders of the sheep, then I will have done you a lasting service. The greatest failure is not that you make a mess of your first pastorate by not knowing enough human psychology, necessary as it is (it is all in the Bible, anyway!). The greatest failure is that you fail to minister the Word of God in any effectiveness or fullness to the people.

The ministers who are the greatest failures are not necessarily those who make such havoc of a church that they have to pass on and leave someone else to put humpty-dumpty together again (for that may mean merely re-establishing the synthesis of the church and the world again), but the greatest failures are those who, having tried to run Christ's church as a moneymaking racket, a clockwork train, or a social free-for-all, depart and leave a spiritual wilderness behind them, in which the one thing that is not known at all is the Word of God.

Dying to Serve

A further word: the whole current of the divine has to pass through you, His servant, and little though you may know what is going on in the hearts of your people at first, there is a great price to be paid for being the 'conductor' of divine truth and power. Change the figure: this is sacrificial power, and you will have to die to release its truth into human hearts. You will have to go down into a new death every time you bring forth God's living Word to the people (2 Cor. 4:12). You will have to die, not only to your own sin, but to self in many of its most seemingly innocent and legitimate aspects. Only then can the death and resurrection power of Jesus Christ be communicated to men, and we dare not do less for any people than this. If we do less, we will have to answer before God one day.

But you may be saying, 'Yes, but when are you going to come to dealing with people individually in their problems?' There are two answers, and the lesser answer I give first. (We will deal with this in more detail in the next chapter.) Take, for instance, hidden problems. Consider what a revelation it may be to those who are truly seeking to live the Christ-life in its vital death and resurrection power, to know that much sin and evil in themselves about which they lament and beat their breasts, is not the mere operation of the principle of inbred sin in your life, but is due to the machinations of a real live devil. He has fastened on their flesh and concealed himself in the folds of their weak human natures so that they go on constantly thrashing themselves for their sinfulness. They never make the self-liberating discovery that there is a devil to be driven out of their lives. Why did Jesus call Peter 'Satan'? This we may learn only from the Word.

Now it may be that such a soul-searching ministry appals you, but read the New Testament and you will see that it is inseparable from a living communication of the Word. God is constantly calling men, tugging, drawing, challenging, chivvying them by the Spirit-winged thrusts of His Word on their consciences, to search themselves in His Presence. It is going on now. There may be division among you about what I am saying. I don't need to know the fact of it, for I know something of the power of the Word to create reaction in human nature, and if I am to help the helpable, I must—rather the Word must—antagonise others, although I must try not to add my own offensiveness to it.

But if dealing with people's problems is all you want, you have missed my point. The real and greater answer is that I have already been dealing with it. Although the Word of God tackles not only obvious problems, but unearths—and ultimately solves—hidden ones too, the real answer is that the living Word thoroughly, adequately and graciously deals with our people, problems and all. Through the death the pastor must die to self, the life of Christ appears in his people.

There it is: Conflict! Cost! Crucifixion! 'Who is sufficient for these things?' None of us. 'Our sufficiency is of God.' But it is when we see the cost of a real work of God in terms of human agony and sacrifice that we see whether our call to the ministry is of God or is a mere romantic notion.

Chapter Two

THE PASTOR OUTSIDE THE PULPIT

The thesis of the earlier talk was that since the pastor is the shepherd of the sheep, his work is to feed and tend them in their need. I said that they were being fed for sacrifice, and it is necessary that they should be free from blemish and pleasing to God. If this work is summed up as the ministry of the whole Word to the whole flock, it is not to say that it is done only in pulpit and rostrum; obviously not, but all the rest follows and flows from the ministry of the Word.

Start with the Word

Look at it like this: the Christ life is Christ in us. Christ is revealed 'in all the scriptures' (Luke 24:27). We can only learn Him there, and become transformed into His image through feeding on His Word. All that many spiritually sick people need is a good, balanced diet and a disciplined routine. My principal surgery, clinic, vestry hour, consulting room—call it what you will—is the pulpit and teaching desk. If, in the end, I cannot get people to see this, I despair of them ever becoming what Christ means them to be; they will certainly never become the satisfied, happy and, more important, useful people they could be. It is through the ministry of the whole Word, every part of it (*e.g.*, I think of the inestimable value of some studies in the book of Proverbs which proved to be an eye-opener as far as the practical details of daily living are concerned)—it is through that ministry that men and women are made and, when they resist it, are marred.

Problem People

One of the great sorrows of my work is that through the years a certain number of persons have collapsed under my ministry because, thinking I was stronger than they, they clung to me in the hope that by climbing on to my back they could become more than it was in them to be, and, therefore, in God's will for them to be. In the end the Word preached, which they came ultimately to hate, broke them; and knowing it was breaking them, they demanded it be changed and turned into a soothing syrup to heal them. It could not be, of course, for even the gentlest word rent them, and when the fantastic beanstalk of unwitting presumption was felled to the ground by the axe-blows of the Word of God, down came the poor Jacks with it; I was blamed for doing irreparable harm to delicate and sensitive personalities. I do not deny my agency in that to some extent and it breaks my heart. But it was the Word that broke them, because they became attached to a personality which had become attractive to them, and which they believed to be fruitful through the livingness of the Word. They did not want the Word itself. My greatest heartbreaks have been with people who, failing to see that it is the Word that brings out the true flavour of personality, wanted to absorb the preacher's personality but not the Word—wanted the fruit but not the root, like people want the ethic without the Cross.

All this has to be faced in the ministry of the Word: nevertheless, it is that ministry which makes Christian character, so that healthy feeders need the pastor less and less. At last they need him no more as clinician or nurse. They have found the solution to their problems and, much more important, have learned to live with those which will only be fully solved in heaven. Now they are able to become, as I said before, pastors to others, to help them solve their problems through the Word.

One's dealings then, with stray, casual, nominal souls, on any other basis than that of a fairly steady and solid diet of the Word of God, are bound to be on a comparatively superficial level: one gives bits of human advice here and there, trying to see life as lived on their level, and no more than challenging them to consider life on a deeper level. Do you see what I mean? You give them the Christian witness, if they will tolerate it at all, but where they don't want it, you do the best you can for them on their own level and leave it there. The Christian minister needs a mental filing cabinet of many drawers, and he is constantly placing, replacing and rearranging people in it. While in one sense he offers only one standard of life, in another sense he can only help people on the level upon which they want help. After all, you will not convert people against their wills, and you will not make people feed their souls on the Word of God against their wills.

Jesus allowed people, when He had challenged them, to choose their level. That is why He let the rich young ruler go. You must discern what people are after, and not waste a lifetime running after those who are vain and empty, selling them a Christ they don't want. Give them the help they ask for, if you can legitimately do so, and probably give them a spiritual dig with it, a challenge—and let them go. For you will find that the ministry of the Word of God by the Spirit not only solves many difficulties, but raises many more, and the most of your time will be spent in helping those who have been faced with new problems through the Word. Many things you cannot say in public, and some things you say generally will need clarification or specific application in private afterwards, to people's personal condition or situation.

But it is not even in the private chats which follow the preaching of the Word that souls are straightened out, so much as in further sitting and listening to the Word. How often people have said that they have spent a week wrestling over some spiritual or moral problem and then, coming to church, have had it all solved in the ministry of the Word. So much so, that many have accused the preacher of preaching at them, or knowing and discussing their private affairs in public. There *have* been times when I have dealt with the problems of individuals in public (anonymously, of course) because they were the problems of others, but more often than not I have been totally unaware that so-and-so was in this difficulty at all. After all, the Holy Spirit has more sense, not to say more care for folk than we have. If only we would trust Him! He will guide us into all the truth, which means, not that we will know everything so that we become walking theological encyclopaedias (Ugh!), but that He will lead us into all the truth we need to know, to live Christ's life to the fullest extent in our personal situation.

At the other extreme from those who regard you as a mere official to perform rites, sign forms, and do bits of peripheral social work not yet catered for by the welfare state, there are those who must not be allowed to devour your time and energy because their problems are beyond you. It is not that they are beyond God. Rather, there are limits to your ability and calling, and, this being a world not only of sin but of the fruits of sin, it is constantly strewn with the wrecks of

God's judgements; that's what ruined lives are. There are some who want their lives sorted out, even by Christ if He will be so kind, and by Christ's minister, too. After all, that's what he is paid for! *By* Christ but not *for* Christ. The whole world wants Christian fruits, but not Christian roots—cut flowers only!

Knowing Our Limitations

It is my view that a great many folk with weak minds and weaker wills have given themselves into the hands of evil powers, not knowing fully what they were letting themselves in for. Having yielded themselves to something which they ought to have known was wrong, sinful, or un-Christlike (what proportion of their plight is due to inheritance and environment, and what to personal wilful perversity, I do not know), they have yielded themselves to this evil until they are thoroughly mixed-up personalities. It has been something of a comfort to me, if not to them, to learn ultimately that Christian psychiatrists, or psychiatrists not anti-Christian, have judged them pretty hopeless cases, with no very good prospects of living useful lives. You may have heard the story of the man who went to the psychiatrist and told him that his problem was an inferiority complex. The psychiatrist did his best with him, and then brutally, perhaps too brutally, gave his considered opinion. 'Your trouble is not inferiority complex,' he said, 'but just that you are plain inferior.' Cruel, but probably true!

There is a lesson there. Some meddling ministers want to sort out everybody. God is not so optimistic. There are some who will die mixed-up personalities, and they may be true believers. (In some ways perhaps I am that, and have no hope of ever sorting myself out. Indeed, my salvation is to live with my oddities and partly put up with them, not to say help other people to put up with them, and partly rise above them to show that grace is better employed wrestling resignedly, realistically, cheerfully with our problems than demanding from God heavenly solutions on earth.) Don't try to do the impossible. Know your limitations, and know what God is seeking to do in the world and what part in it He wants you to play. Think of the mess the world is in. Supposing there were gods in other universes, and our God was showing them round His one and telling them what His Son came to do two thousand years ago, He would have a pretty red face, wouldn't He, if He showed them the earth only, and not the masses of glorified saints in heaven.

You may ask, 'What of Christ's miraculous healing and restoring powers?' I know, but, as we were saying, Jesus turned away from that ministry to teach His disciples. I believe that He was showing forth, in a good sense—even showing off(!)—the perfect works of His kingdom and the ideal characters men were to become when His kingdom came. We know that Christ can 'sort out' every soul. Why does He not do it? Is the failure the church? Did Jesus fail with Judas? Does God fail when the unbelieving are cast into the hell of their own choosing along with the horrible of the earth and of the demon world? Know what God is about, especially in respect of your calling, and keep within it. Most people crack up because they try to do what God never intended them to do. They destroy themselves by sinful ambition, just as much as the drunkard and drug addict. Ambition drives them on.

It is most important to try to discover with difficult spiritual and psychological cases whether their problems are beyond you or not, and if they are, to leave them to others better equipped and qualified. I have spent many gruelling hours through the years with those who have nearly broken me, of whom it has been said at last by better authorities than I, that they were not very hopeful cases. Not that they would be useless in society, but that their problems were too deeply ingrained, too innate for full solution on earth, at least with our present knowledge. I am far more ready now to give up with difficult people than I used to be, and hand them over to those better fitted to deal with them. And some of these are now doing good service within certain limits, although their friends may not know that they are full of problems inside, and so will be happy enough to live and work with them. But they are not what ambitious evangelical ardour had hoped they would become. With fuller understanding, and taking a leaf out of Christ's own Book, we become more realistic about people.

The Consultant Pastor

Learning to pass on to professional carers cases which are beyond the pastor's ability to help enables him to concentrate upon real pastoral work, supplementary and complementary to the public ministry, for then he is not dealing with those who are torn with irreconcilable, inner conflicts but with those who wholeheartedly want

Christ, and want to live the Christ-life fully, in the church and in the world. The will to do is half the battle. Our help to such is largely to clarify, specify and apply the publicly ministered Word to their particular total situation. Here is where the so-called 'consultant pastor' comes into his own.

It is important to make it known that you lay yourself out for this. If you are not holding down a little church merely until you get a big one, but really care for people, at least as much as you care for your own wife and children, then you must convey to them a real awareness that you are interested in their problems. If you are not interested in the problems of sincere, ongoing Christians you ought not to be in the work of ministry at all.

Of course, you have to deal faithfully with those who are attracted to you and want to be that little bit farther in with you than their sparring partners, and you will have to deal with those who like attention and who manufacture problems, or even excuses, to draw inconsiderately on your time. Some even love to see a queue waiting to speak to you after a service and maliciously drag out their story to keep others waiting. But, remember, when you are brokenhearted about the sheer cussedness of some, and bitterness, enmities, jealousies, grudges and feuds seem to rock the boat, remember that, in time—you don't need to go out of your way to dot Mrs Brazenface on the nose from the pulpit!—in time, it will all be dealt with by the systematic preaching of the Word. The answer to every problem, even the ones that have no full and final earthly solution, is in the Word. Pin your faith to that. Let the Word solve or settle all.

Listening

When real people come seeking real help, receive them with all grace, patience and forbearance. Let them talk: don't jump to conclusions and turn the interview into another sermon on the lines they may have heard many times before. If they are real, they know all that. But there may be something that has not been made plain so far, at least to them. Let them talk, and you listen.

The hardest thing ministers, who are great talkers, find to do is to listen. Don't be making up your next speech while the other is talking. Listen! You may hear something you have never heard before. Don't assume that this problem is like many others you have dealt with. It may seem to be, but as no two people are exactly alike, so no two persons' problems are alike. You will find that many of your fixed ideas, which you may think are thoroughly Christian and apply to all cases, will be upset if you listen carefully enough to begin to see what the solution to a particular problem may be.

The most you should allow yourself at first, is to ask questions. Never be tempted to pronounce until you think you have received answers to all the questions you need fully to apprise you of the situation. Ask questions to eliminate possible causes of the trouble, which you may not think are the real cause. Try to get the whole story out, and as you hear it, try to rearrange it, as a mechanic would a heap of iron that he believes includes the essential parts of a car.

I had a young professional man, whose health is not good (in fact, it is a miracle he ever got through his course), visit me some time ago, and he was considering what his calling was to be. He was not able for hard work, yet wanted to work among people, not do research. Would he go abroad? Was this a romantic, escapist notion? After going into the whole case pretty thoroughly it was obvious that he should not run away from all the people in the fellowship who really cared for him. He could not undertake hard work—so it had to be research. He had pretty well come to that conclusion (I knew he wanted only God's will and God's best for his life): all he needed from me was confirmation and help to put away the romantic notion of going abroad, or of hoping to do a strong man's job. Now, I might have ruined that life as he trusted me, had I not waited patiently to see what God was saying to him in his situation.

Common Sense

So much of God's will is just Christian common sense when we are prepared to see it sanely. Very often all that people want is to think their problems through in your hearing and come with you to the obvious conclusion. Let us not underestimate the healing, stabilising effect of what I call the 'Confidential'—others call it the 'Confessional'! There are times, of course, when after such an interview you may see that there is a warp in your patient's thinking.

I had been 'going at it' one Sunday evening about living your whole life in Christ and for Christ, and one chap, because he thought that I must live my life on my knees, came to me, wringing his hands, because he was not being as holy as he thought he ought to be. I said to him, 'You foolish boy, do you think this means winding yourself up into a kind of robot existence, forever clicking your heels before a ruthless sergeant-major Christ? You have got it all wrong. Christ is a world of being, not a set of rules. You live your life in Him, you are naughty in him, alas, as well as good in Him. You have fun there as well as seriousness. You must learn that Christ is no mere censor, but a Saviour who saves us by gaining our trust and confidence more and more, and letting us live our total life in Him. He is much more concerned about where we are going, than about how far on we have got.'

This chap's Christ was a drill sergeant and he thought that was what I was advocating. No: I was thinking of a Christ who would be with him when he went off the deep end and betrayed his fallen self and made an ass of himself, and, in private, denied his own, true, holy nature. A Christ who was always kindly, always there, not to his sin, but to him. Who was willing to be dragged to places and into thoughts that He hated, because He loved him and would not let him go. Who at the most would say, 'Tut, tut,' or, 'I told you so,' or, 'That won't work and you know it, but have your fling,' or, 'You are a chump, when will you learn?' Well, none of this you can say from a pulpit, at least, not as you can say it personally. I had to reassure him that there were certain limitations to public preaching, and Christians needed to know one another in more informal circumstances to see how the intense and absolute things one said so fervently in public are not incompatible, but complementary, to those of the more informal life, social and private.

There is a plus about the Spirit's personal teaching of the Word in church which is quite different from, albeit does not contradict the other life. Mind you, I think that a preacher must show what he is, more and more, in his preaching; even his humour cannot be excluded, although like Christ's, it must be restrained because of the grimness of the battle against sin and evil. But if his preaching is not to be a 'performance' (what a sin it is to stand up there like a little god, when you are nothing of the kind), he must see to it that his whole personality is poured into it. Yet, even so, there is another life, perhaps two or three other lives, not incompatible, inconsistent, double or hypocritical, but just different; yet still the real 'you'. And still lived in the presence of Christ, although not in the same high-powered way as in a church service or meeting. This doesn't split the personality, but rather integrates its various legitimately different strands.

Building a Fellowship

Which leads me to this point. Next to the ministry of the Word, the most fruitful pastoral duty is to help all sorts of odd sheep to live together, and show them how to live in the world amongst goats without becoming goats. One of the great lessons of Paul's letter to the Ephesians is how the saints should fit in together. The greatest sin there is to refuse to fit in, and want to stick out like a sore thumb, drawing attention to oneself. Some have to be shown by the Word, and in private conversation, that soul-cure is largely a matter of learning to live and worship together. The testimony of a true Christian church ought to be how Christians love one another including the 'odd bods'. Christ likes odd bods. I sometimes say that nearly all the fruitful Christian ministers, and fruitful laymen I know, are odd bods. But they are odd bods with a mission, a mission to fit other odd bods, along with themselves, into a fellowship.

Never countenance as legitimate the claim of any to stand out from a fellowship. No! No! They may have great intellects or may have titles and pedigrees a thousand years long, that is of no importance. I have seen a family tree five-foot long and I have 'climbed' up it, lying on a very super Wilton carpet, but the lady in question just fits in with all the rest in the fellowship and receives the same care and treatment as the dear woman who was once her maid. The same, but different, of course. Happily both not only accept, but revel in this situation, for they know that they are of equal value to God.

Visiting

Now, a word about visiting. There has to be a certain amount of social visiting, I suppose. But, as a spiritual ministry progresses, the demand for worthwhile pastoral ministry becomes so great that the merely social has to be left out more and more. Happy is the minister who has trained his congregation not to expect to see him unless there is particular need, and who, when there is need, don't try to keep him in the dark as long as possible so that they may ostentatiously reproach him when he does find out. Happy is the minister whose people release him from petting and pampering them, so that he can get on with the real work of building the church, seeking the lost, patiently encouraging others to persevere, and sharing the sorrows, sicknesses, loneliness and heartbreaks of those who are in real need.

In visiting, the extremes are that one may try to do too much in a visit, or too little. I think that one of the greatest mistakes Christians, and particularly Christian ministers make, is to underestimate the presence and working of the Holy Spirit in their lives. When you visit a home, God enters it, or should. This doesn't mean that you instantly begin to pontificate or preach. When Jesus met the woman of Samaria, He asked a drink from her, and so the conversation unfolded, and a revival followed! Christ can be known in the homeliest things, can proceed with His work and can be drawn out to do it from the homeliest beginnings. Indeed, He does not need to draw attention to Himself at all. Some people gain the strength they need from their minister by his calling to see how they are, making a few homely remarks, and going his way without any attempt at what some would call pastoral ministration. Some of you will not agree with this, but that does not disturb me.

Indeed, my whole view of the Christian's responsibility for primary evangelism is founded upon the belief that the greatest evangelistic and pastoral agency in the world is the Holy Spirit dwelling naturally in God's children, so that Christ shines out of them all the time—or nearly all the time—and is known to do so by those with whom they have anything more than casual contact, and even with them. We have to let our light shine—not hide it, and certainly not flash it, which draws attention to ourselves—and we must believe that it is shining. Now and then comes the opportunity to let its beam blaze out like a lighthouse, as some need is made known, or we are challenged as to our faith. But, normally, we let the light shine, believing that Jesus Christ is witnessing through us, in and to the world. This can happen better in the home than in some places. I had a meal with some humble folk a few weeks ago, and because they were brought up as I was, I chatted to them in broad Scots, which is my native tongue. When I had gone, one of them said, 'What a plain man the minister is.' They did not think less of me for being on their level. Christ never gave Himself airs. Why should we? It is all a question of what we are trying to do.

As a pastor, will you be merely trying to do a job and fulfil a duty, or will you be letting Christ in human flesh through to the people you are mixing with? If the latter, then it is the easiest thing in the world. You simply be what you are in Christ, no more, and no less, and let that speak. If Christ is not concerned to be sanctimonious (and He certainly was not sanctimonious with the woman of Samaria), do you think you can do better by being self-consciously unctuous? If Christ has given you a love for people (and what are you doing in this work if He has not?), then the fact of it is the important thing, not the showing off of it. People have misunderstood me for years because I would not dance their evangelistic jigs and utter their clichés and shibboleths, and observe all their polite conventions. But when they were in real need, it was not a matter then of showing what was in me, or what I was made of, but of responding to their need as distinct from their conventional repartee, and being seen for what I was. Far better, surely, than being thought to be such a nice man, and then being found out! Grace and truth come by Jesus Christ.

This is what should be seen in our normal visiting. Far better that someone should ask for a word of prayer, or a reading, than that one should leave a trail of forced readings and prayers in a number of homes where it was not convenient, or where people were sorely embarrassed, or annoyed, and didn't want them. I am never put out, although some who ask me hope that I may, by being asked to pray in a home. 'We had to ask him to pray: he doesn't know the first thing about his job'! In such a house they get a poor prayer. Who could pray in that atmosphere? I daren't pray what I think which is, 'Lord, would you deal with this self-righteous lot who love to take the minister down a peg by showing how pious they are.' To visit such people is a pain, and one hopes that sooner or later the Word will get under their skin and they will be humbled. But in other homes one's whole soul cries out to speak with the Lord, and we are instantly in heaven and speaking of Him and to Him, and seeing our common life in His gentle light. This is particularly true when there is bereavement, or at a funeral service, as equally when there is joy. You can bring all the tender heart of Jesus Christ to bear on needy souls and know that He Himself is ministering to them through you.

It goes without saying that one takes in the situation in any home when one arrives, and does not force oneself on people at an inconvenient moment, or stay on if one senses that one is interrupting plans or is really in the way. Sometimes the Lord arranges that people are out when you call, and you pop a card through the letter-box, and this is all that they may need to arrest them, correct them, or assure them that they are not forgotten, and so you get on to somewhere else where you may be more needed.

On the other hand, you may visit homes where there is real need and there may be little evidence of it. They may be stiff, shy, introverted folk who need to have things dragged out of them. You must learn the art of asking leading, direct, even shock questions, perhaps catching the over-composed ones off their guard, and then, greatly daring, but with a sure, unerring touch, barging right in and cracking them open, as if to say 'Come off it. There's a bit of a muddle here. Why don't you admit it, and let's get on with the clearing up.'

On one occasion I had a hint from one of our senior boys that a certain young student had been floored, humbled, and at last would be coming to see me. I was glad because he had been with us eighteen months and although he had not got on very well academically, any time we had been in conversation, even in my home he always said—sitting primly on the edge of a chair—that he was getting on well. He was such a pious little fellow, cocky, bouncy and facile: I found him a bit of a humbug and used to long for him to go. Well, my senior boy, who is near his age, cracked him open one day, and he collapsed in a heap and admitted how miserable he was, and how afraid he was that he would be cast off if he admitted it. I said to him, 'This cocky act of yours did not deceive. I don't assume that everybody on the face of the earth is "Getting on fine, thank you", and all they have to do in life is to put other people right. So that the more you gave yourself airs, the more sure I was that you were a fraud, acting a part. And you were so unattractive like that. Don't you know that sinners are the only kind of men Jesus can love? Remember how He sent the Pharisees packing until only the woman taken in adultery was left standing with Him? I don't believe you thought you would be cast off if you admitted you were a nasty little mess inside. You were just trying to make yourself believe that you were that rather wonderful image you tried to project.'

In certain company you dare not let people know what you are, but amongst Jesus-folk, within reason and in degree according to how Jesus-minded they are, you can and must. A true Christian fellowship is a place where stray cats and dogs can find a home. It is a hospital, where the only sin is to hide your wounds from the doctor and nurse. And the true pastor's job is to strip all the fearful ones, however gently, patiently, faithfully, and all the hypocritical ones of their camouflage and cloaks. Grace and truth come by Jesus Christ.

Artificial Stratagems

A word about meddlesome attempts to get you to convert persons who are brought to you out of the blue. Every autumn I have a spate of letters from fond parents, teachers, guardians and monitors, appealing to me to follow up such-and-such a youngster who is away from home at College for the first time, and who has to be hunted, followed, shadowed, intercepted and driven to Christian meetings. I have scarcely ever known this desperate technique to work. I understand the panic of parents and guardians, but it is too late then to try high-pressure tactics. Prayer, example and precept, in that order, are the means of bringing up children and young folk in the faith. Nor will high-pressure tactics and brainwashing techniques avail when young folk have gone off on their own. Some young folk, alas, will have their fling and sow their wild oats, and come at last to heel, sadly, like the prodigal son. It is where Christians pathetically put their trust in external techniques and artificial stratagems that young folk go astray. Nothing takes the place of the realism of holy living and secret wrestling before God in prayer for our youngsters. We must commit them to God so utterly that we dare not interfere or tamper with their precious souls.

It is also very exasperating when someone brings along another and lays him at your feet as if to say, 'Convert him.' Or someone sends you to hospital to convert a dying person. A very fine lad came to see me some time ago about a fellow student he had 'digged' with for more than a year. I was going out and could not stay to chat, but bade him return next day which he did, complete with the chap in question. There we were, the three of us, and with the merest introduction, I was expected to get out my tools and start on the fellow right away.

My fine Christian friend lolled back in his chair—my chair!—as if he were to watch a television show of some delicate operation. 'Well, well,' I said to myself, 'you are in for a shock.' I proceeded to put the new fellow off, supposing that although these two had talked a lot together over the year, he was not interested enough to have his whole life transformed. I made it sound as exacting as I could, told him that if he was really interested it would be shown by his coming to church (he had hardly ever been), and taking the whole thing in and appraising it thoroughly. I told him if he came he must come with all his critical faculties wide awake and he must say to himself, 'Now, what's going on here? Is this a farce, or is there a real God here? If so, what is He saying, and are these people really in touch with Him, and is He really speaking to me too?' My friend looked askance but said nothing, and I showed them out.

That was not the first one that had been converted by being shown, rather curtly, to the door! Sure enough, there was the bold hero in church on Sunday morning and back in the evening. The following Sunday he was back again with another pal of his. He has been coming ever since, a month or two, but only once a Sunday now. I don't know if he will 'take'. That is not

my affair, much as I would do anything to win
him.

What does it profit if, by specious and
plausible means, we gather a whole lot of folk
around us who are not converted to Christ at all,
or are only half-baked, because we are afraid to
turn the heat on them? Let us have reality above
all things in this business of pastoral work. Let us
turn the white light of the all-searching eye of
God upon men and let Him sift and search them
out, and then let His love draw them. Then let us
feed them on the 'finest of the wheat', building
them up, until God thrusts them out into His
harvest fields. This is how His work is done,
fruitfully and lastingly.

But, remember, the pastor is not a spiritual
doctor. The tension in his work is between the
ministry of the Word and the guiding of the soul.
The Holy Spirit is the Doctor. The work is done
through a 'dead man' ministering the living Word
in the power of the Spirit, wooed into the midst
by the prayers of the saints. It is only the 'fiddly'
bits that are done in private, because a soul is
never so much in private with God as when
sitting in church being sifted, searched, corrected,
fed and nourished by the ministry of the Word.
Pin your faith to that, and the God who gives you

grace to do it fruitfully will easily train you to deal with 'fiddly' bits in private, and cause you to know your limitations in the doing of it too.

Chapter Three

COMPLETE AND
CONTEMPORARY

I have two things to say in this chapter. The first is that our ministry is that of the Word of God, which is eternal and abides for ever (1 Pet. 1:23–5). The second is that the eternal Word of God is ever contemporary. We hear people talking about Christ our Contemporary, and He is; but that is because His eternal Spirit is contemporary in the world and makes the Book in which He is revealed, contemporary. As to the first, I have not a great deal to say about the Word as eternal and abiding for ever. I hope it is obvious to you. To the second—that the Word is ever contemporary—I want to say that the Word as ministered in the manner and setting of other ages, without contemporary application, is doubly unsuitable to our age, in that it speaks to a bygone age and therefore fails to speak to our own.

More than 'Gospel'

To the first. You will notice I have not spoken of the ministry of the Gospel but of the Word of God, and this I do advisedly. It is not that I want to avoid the word 'Gospel', but because I want you to be very sure what I am talking about. I am not talking about a set of fundamental doctrines of the Word of God, systematic or otherwise, nor any formulation of doctrine (sub-Apostolic, Patristic, Reformed or Modern) culled from the Word of God, but the whole Bible itself. In evangelical circles the danger that the Gospel may be equated with the mere rudiments of the Word of God has become almost a disaster, for these rudiments are only the beginning of the Good News. There are profounder things by far in the Bible than what is called 'the simple Gospel', although they issue from it. Indeed, in a sense, those who proclaim almost exclusively forgiveness of sins and justification, only make known the preliminaries to the best Good News, which is not that our sins are put away and that we are justified in God's sight, wonderful though that is, but that God wants us for Himself and to that end brings us to the birth in Christ. After all, the death of Jesus, for all its wonder, is a means to an end, which is not merely that we may be right and clean but that we may be His, which involves personal relationship in love.

(You will find, by the way, that doctrinal formulations of the truth of the Word of God generally set the forgiveness of sins and justification before sanctification; but, of course, in objective fact, the *new birth* is first because, being the greatest, it embraces the less, and all the rest; see Eph. chs 1 and 2.)

Beyond the deeper truths of the Gospel—which, alas, so many do not teach and preach for, I fear, reasons obscure to others but known to themselves—there is the darker backcloth to the Good News, namely, the penal and corrective judgements of God, upon which the scintillating diamond of the Gospel shines with a thousand facets. The judgements are also the Word of God; and only he who preaches and teaches the whole Bible, dark and light, rightly dividing the Word of truth, fully proclaims the Word of God. After all, we see a rainbow only on the clouds.

This raises many questions which could keep us for hours, particularly the question: 'How do you preach and teach the whole Bible?' But, lest we range too widely, all I will say now is that once you are convinced your people need—I say need—the whole Word of God, and you get over the shock to your indolent flesh that you are not in the ministry for an easy job, you simply roll up your sleeves, and, having gathered, or being in process of gathering, the most helpful library of commentaries and reference books you can find, you get down to it: and book by book you give your people a balanced diet of the truth.

To those who fear (and they are many) that the simple Gospel will get lost in the process, let me say that evangelism is not merely a matter of words. There is the Spirit, and if He is present in the Word, do you not think He will use the Word to deal faithfully with all who hear, so that the thoughts of many hearts may be revealed? Therefore, as you teach and preach your way through the Word, your people will hear many things, both good news and bad, that they never dreamt were in the Bible at all.

The Whole Word

Is it not a serious charge made against many that in the course of years of ministry there is not one book of the Bible thoroughly ransacked and explored? Having preached and taught my way through all the books of the Bible several times, and through the New Testament books many times, I never come to a fresh exposition without feeling that I am coming to something new. And one invariably sees it in some new light, or in some new relation to the whole Word. To keep dipping away into our own pet subjects and giving folk what we like best, or they like best, is not the way to feed the flock. No school teacher would get away for long with that cavalier attitude to the curriculum. If we are called at all, it is to the ministry of the whole Word of God. Why, the New Testament itself drives us back to the Old, and the various divisions of each Testament drive us to the others, to supplement and complement our knowledge.

Incidentally, you will find that as you range through the whole Bible at the Spirit's behest, thrilling at ever fresh discoveries, you will become more and more convinced of the unity of the whole Book. For instance, it's quite something to find Paul in Romans and Galatians turning to Genesis chapters 12, 15, 17 to preach the Gospel, and showing God's promise to Abraham before the Law was enjoined through Moses; and Jesus in the marriage question turning back to Genesis 2; and seeing the ground plan of Ezekiel's city standing as a kind of mid-pillar of a bridge which joins the garden of Eden to the heavenly city of Revelation 22.

We must, of course, begin where it began. We must take pains to try to know and understand its various historical settings. Yet we must not get lost, or get the Word itself lost in its setting. Do not be like the preacher who was so full of the historical description of the armour in Ephesians 6 that it became a history lesson and the mighty dynamic of a terrific passage was lost. We must learn to deal faithfully with the Bible's history, and understand the background to the giving of the Law, to the prophets, and to the sacred writings, before we begin to 'Christianise' them—as Christianise them we must, by bringing them under the control of the New Testament.

You will hear it said sometimes that you must not try to read the New Testament into the Old. Well, that may be well meant. It is possible to misread the New Testament into the Old, but what about Peter's words (1 Pet. 1:10–12), that the Old Testament prophets themselves did not fully understand the words they were given, or what they pointed to. They spoke more fully and deeply than they knew. The New Testament itself reads into the Old, but not without respect to it, and not without knowledge of the Old Testament settings themselves. The Epistle to the Hebrews is the classical example of this.

Preaching <u>Today's</u> Word

The second thing I have to say is that the Word of God, for all that it is embedded in the pages of ancient history, is yet a contemporary jewel. It is the ever living Word of God—when the living Spirit who gave it is, by the sanctified human mind, kept trained upon its truth. All the spiritual archaeologist needs to do to discover its dazzling brightness is to take the trouble to brush or blow away a little archaic dust from it to make it shine in its own undimmed and undimmable glory. The Word of God to have effect must be preached and taught contemporarily, not as an old-fashioned thing. Its treasures, which are old, are ever new, and it is all-important to see this.

Certainly we must seek to learn what Christian scholars through the ages have thought and said about the Word which we are called to expound and proclaim. But we must be careful not to cart out of their volumes the applications which they made of the Word which had peculiar relevance to their own day, else we will be preaching to men long since dead, and to a situation that has changed out of all recognition.

It is strange that we find far more preachers in the sixteenth and seventeenth centuries than in the first. But whether our one scholarly foot is in the first or sixteenth century AD, or the sixth or tenth century BC, our other dynamical foot must be firmly planted in our own day. We must not live in any other century, year, month or day than the present. While we must teach and preach the perennially contemporary Word of God from its historical settings, we are teaching and preaching it in the present day and it must be bang up to date.

Not Sixteenth Century

Take, for instance, someone who believes that the support the German princes gave to Martin Luther's cause was necessary to the advance of the

Reformation, or that Calvin's city state (part of which he owed to those who had gone before) was the essential end of the ministry of the Word of God and that the purpose of the Word of God is to build Christian states on earth. Such a person will join wholeheartedly with churchmen who dabble in politics, thinking this is the task of the Christian minister, and will find himself out with Romans 13:1–7 and 1 Peter 2:12–14 (and context). He will be sidetracked from the real work which is to evangelise the community and edify the church, not Christianise the state.

We take for granted our liberty to proclaim the Gospel and worship God in our land as we wish, but we are not promised that liberty in the New Testament at all. Indeed the day may come, even in our time, when it may be taken away. Christian churches often thrive best (New Testament-wise) when their human liberty is jeopardised. Certainly, we shall never Christianise the state; more fool we, if we think we can, or that we have done so.

Listen to what the late Lt. Col. Thomson, a retired senior official of the Foreign Office, said about Christians and the state. (He had travelled extensively in Eastern Europe and Russia and went through these countries twice a year encouraging and helping Christian groups.)

> Our Lord Jesus Christ never promised to His followers unrestricted liberty to do precisely what they wanted; on the contrary, He told them to expect tribulation in this world. The best they could hope for was mere toleration; they were not to marvel if the world hated them. No question of diplomatic protests or pressures, dispatch of warships, imposition of boycotts, or the like. In those days they were strangers and pilgrims of the type we now see behind the Iron Curtain, but very seldom on our side of it.

A great many of us are far busier propping up our particular brand of democracy and social service than building the church of Jesus Christ against which even the gates of hell shall not prevail, whether our democracy collapses or not. The church is not called to subsidise the state any more than she is called to work against it; she has to be as neutral to it as loyal citizens can be. She is called to gather and build the church of Jesus Christ under any system whatsoever. Her members are to submit to the powers that be, as far as this does not conflict with the individual conscience, and they are to let the state do as it will. If the state forbids Christians, loyal Christians, to be Christians, she can only kill the body, she cannot kill the soul. What Paul and Peter are saying in Romans 13:1–7 and l Peter 2 is that we are to submit to whatever regime we happen to be under—submit to it, not sponsor, or oppose it.

We are supposed to believe that there are no conditions on earth in which the Christian church cannot survive, for God will always see to it that the blood of the martyrs is the seed of the church that is to be. That is certainly true beyond the Iron Curtain. When Lt. Col. Thomson wanted the richest Christian fellowships he could find, he went for them to Poland, Czechoslovakia, Hungary, Yugoslavia, Romania and Russia. He told us of a young man who was converted in the Red Army. You will not read of that in Investia or Pravda, but it is so, none the less. Do not think that the church is smothered in these countries. She is more likely to be smothered by wealth, ease and complacency.

Have you ever thought why the world knew a thousand years of darkness after Christ came, and why Mohammed came six hundred years after Christ? If you want a pin-point (I admit it sounds naive, but is it so untrue?), take Constantine bringing the Christian church under the wing of the state: 'the greatest single disaster ever to overtake the Christian church'.[1] That is why the interference in the Rhodesian affair by Dr Ramsey (the then Archbishop of Canterbury), was so bad; not necessarily for what he said (who will be a judge of that ticklish situation?), but because as a leader of the Christian church he spoke on that subject at all. Neither our Lord, nor the Apostles would have been so foolhardy. When the members of the Sanhedrin sought to trip up Jesus on a political question, He gave one of the most guarded and diplomatic, and yet one of the most searching answers in history: 'Render unto Caesar the things that are Caesar's, and unto God the things that are God's.' The Apostles were none the less wise. Read their speeches in the Acts and observe their needle-point. It is not calculated diplomacy, but simply that they were so burned up with one thing that they could not be distracted or sidetracked by any other.

Now you cannot disagree with my examples from our Lord and the Apostles. If you disagree with me about Dr Ramsey and others today, I have only one rejoinder: it is to ask the question, 'How did Christianity abolish slavery?' Have we a charter in the New Testament for deliberately setting out to abolish it? Not a word. That's a sidetrack. Why? Is the New Testament in favour of slavery? Not at all, but it is not to be sidetracked trying to achieve what can only be achieved by Christians becoming their true selves in the church and in the world, and letting that influence work itself into society. All that is good, namely, the abolition of slavery, the founding of hospitals, educational institutions, social services, the emancipation of women, *etc.,* flows from that, and to be right, the Christian church as such—certainly, those called to the ministry of the Word of God and prayer—should never be sidetracked by these things. They are the by-products of the church being the church in the world.

If you are acquainted with the nineteenth-century Christian social reformers, Shaftesbury, Barnardo, *etc.*, you will know that they did not drag their social reforms into the church, or desert the church for them, or even neglect it to pursue them. What burned brightest in their hearts was not love to man, but love to God. That is why their love to man was so sure and fruitful. They went out from the church to make their country better, but they did not leave the church, as so many social reformers in our day have done. The church and its worship was to them always more than their social work. It was the inspiration and springboard of all their good works.

We don't get character like that very much today. The church and its ministry, alas, do not breed it. Because of the nationalisation of the church under Constantine, and the institutionalisation of it subsequently, she has failed to see that as a remnant church, gathering and building up a hidden Kingdom in an ever alien world, she is always in a missionary situation. The hope of the Christianisation of the state, or even the Christianisation of a complete community, is vain. (Albeit mighty revivals have put a stamp upon communities which has remained for generations.) The state nationalises the church; equally disastrously, the church sets herself over the state in a wrong way, that is, in a way of temporal power like Becket, and defies it. Feed, I pray you, on the insights into the Word of God of the Reformers, and of all other great men of the church, but have nothing to do with their optimistic hopes of Christianising this world, whether you call it with Augustine a city of God, or with Calvin a city state. The only One who will establish that ideal order is the Lord Jesus Christ Himself at His coming.

Does someone say, 'Do you not want the church to make impacts on the state?' With all my heart: but not that way. Her influence is indirect, not direct, and is always most powerful when she is attending to her own work, which is building the Kingdom of God. Look at it this way. Is it not most discouraging to the betterment of the world that when we have begun to get people's lives half-right, and they have learned the wisdom of how to live together in amity and brotherly love, they die and leave it impoverished, and we have to begin again with a new generation? Is that discouraging? It shouldn't be. All the departing saints are placed in the divine repository until the number is complete, and then all that Kingdom will come, with its King. The church's impacts upon society are almost a by-product—if you can call a word of judgement on the ungodly a by-product. But all its by-products are to the end that the church may be gathered, and may grow, and that the saints may be massed in heaven. The world is for the church, not the church for the world.

Not Seventeenth Century

Perhaps your temptation is not to live in the sixteenth century, or in the world of its discoveries or impacts: you prefer the seventeenth century. It may be that even now you are in process of absorbing not only the solid teaching of the Puritan writers, and therefore acquiring the stable character those teachings inculcate. But you may be seeing the Word of God through their eyes in such a way that you are really living three hundred years ago, and have acquired a detachment from the present day, and even a cold disdainful attitude towards it that makes you exceedingly unattractive and forbidding. What a pity. For this tendency in you will increase, because, while your love for Puritans and Puritanism is likely to grow as you become absorbed with them and it, the Spirit of God will not bless you in this as He blessed these dear godly men in it. They were dealing with live situations and were making impacts upon them, whereas you are just a dealer in antiques. The last thing in the world the Spirit of God will do is bless those living out of their own age. Some are big enough to absorb a great deal of Puritan teaching because they can do so quickly, and life is short. Yet they remain 'on the ball' of their own day. But many more get lost in the process.

Indeed, to go further back: one of the most difficult problems in reading the New Testament is to weigh the quotations from the Old Testament and see what the New Testament writers make of them. The Old Testament is not a bundle of antiquities, but the living Word of God written and spoken in another day, and taken and made to speak in intelligent contemporary terms to the apostolic day. It is all very well to be taken up with the truth, and to keep repeating that the truth is the thing, but we must never forget that the truth, spoken, written, lived without the living Spirit of God, is asleep. It is dormant.

This is where extreme Neo-Puritanism seems to have gone wrong, as has hidebound Brethrenism in other circles. It has seen the Word of God as solid chunks of the rock of truth to be quarried and laid heavily one upon another to form massive structures, edifices of truth, and even to form bricks to throw at others. Whereas the truth is not the truth, however sound it be, if it is not made molten, fluid fire flowing into hearts by the living, present Spirit of Grace.

The letter kills. Kills! How terrible! Some of the moaning presentations of the truth by lugubrious souls bent on recapturing the spirit of awful repentance vouchsafed to the seventeenth century and now offered to God as the bribe-price of revival, are a pain in the neck. Such say they want revival but that it can come only by such an excess of mournful solemnity as is bound to appal any soul who knows the 'solid joys and lasting treasure' that 'none but Zion's children know.' No joy: what kind of a religion is that? Read Andrew Bonar's diary and you will soon be depressed by his preoccupation with his own sin. Yet his daughter said, I understand, that in the home they knew nothing of that. The goodness of God can and is intended to lead men to repentance.

I have lately seen a young man, happily married, who, upon the birth of his second child, was so bowed down before the Lord with the weight of the Lord's goodness to him because he had sought to go God's way, that his heart was made exceedingly sensitive to sin because it was exceedingly sensitive to God's goodness and love. Whereas some of the present day seventeenth-century 'boys' manage to compose their faces to look like morose old men—not a bit like some of the seventeenth-century divines themselves, if you had seen them romping at home with their children. This may be away from the point, but I remember G. D. Henderson telling us of Karl Barth in his home about fifty-five years ago now. Henderson came in one day to find Barth rolling on the floor with the Henderson boys, more of a child than either of them. I often think of this when I think of Barth.

Some of the present-day seventeenth-century boys wear clothes even to match. A laddie was converted one Christmas Eve in our place on the eve of his departure to the big city. I advised him of two places to worship. Next time he came home he had become a very cold, supercilious 'fish', critical of everyone and everything; the time after that he was dressed from head to foot in black (his shirt apart) and he looked like 'death warmed up'—but not very much! What an artificial, melancholic piece of humbug. Away with it: it is an offence. The Spirit of God is not within a million miles of people like that, in their lives, or in their preaching.

Not Eighteenth Century

Perhaps you do not live in the seventeenth century, but in the eighteenth. You are a Wesley man, and see everything not only from his point of view, but from the point of view of his day. You have a class-meeting complex. I was a Methodist organist for some years and loved these people and would say nothing against them, but their idea seemed to be that the Bible had to be interpreted and the church run on Wesleyan lines and terms. Even if some saw the equivalent degree of spiritual impact to that of Wesley made upon our day in a different denominational setting, they would dismiss it, or by-pass it. 'It is not the way the early Methodists did it: it cannot be right!'

Not Nineteenth Century

But maybe that isn't your trouble. You live in the early nineteenth century, and have acquired the Free Presbyterianism (I mean the spirit, not the denomination) of my native Scotland. What you will be in process of doing is taking the whole Bible and filing it down to one fine point, like a pyramid, cone, or spinning top, so that you can poise the whole on one all-important, all-exclusive and all-inclusive point, namely, the Sabbath Day. This is the whole law; there is no other. You can sin as much as you like against all the other nine commandments, outwardly and inwardly, as long as you preserve twenty-four hours of the week inviolate of any constructive activity, vacuous of any creative purpose, and certainly devoid of any joy. Then do what you like for the rest of the week! You are God's man 'par excellence', nor is there any man like you in heaven or on earth!

But have I still missed the mark? You are not tarred with any of those brushes, although you are very much in the nineteenth century. You don't know very much about the early days of that century in Scotland and about the disruption, about Thomas Chalmers, Murray McCheyne or the Bonars. Your Elysian Fields are the 1859 revival, and in the work of those who came from America about fourteen years later. You are a Moody and Sankey man. Not Moody without Sankey, but definitely Moody *and* Sankey. This is your whole world. This, you believe, is what the Bible is about. At least it is the only thing in the Bible that is worth talking about, or propagating. I tell you, this is still the whole Christian and evangelical world to far too many Christians in Scotland—especially in the Glasgow area—and in Northern Ireland. There is no other. And they are all eighty to ninety years out of date. They are, if you will allow me to say so reverently, wooing the Holy Spirit of the last quarter of the nineteenth and first quarter of the twentieth century, and there isn't such a Holy Spirit. He has moved on past the second and third quarters of the twentieth century, and is now well on into the final quarter. He is pushing ahead so fast that live Christians are hard put to it to catch up with Him.

I can hear you saying, 'Who paid this man to denounce the Protestant ages?' Well, I'm coming to that. I once heard Iain Murray of the Banner of Truth Trust making distinction between Kennedy of Dingwall (Northern Scotland) having Spurgeon to preach in his church when he would not have Moody, whereas Andrew Bonar blessed both the '59 revival and Moody. We must be careful here, as I am sure Iain Murray was. While I cannot in my ignorance be a judge of these matters, there is no doubt at all that the influences in the second half of the nineteenth century which turned the solid Free Church of Scotland into a mere evangelistic mission have been (although their immediate fruits were rich and many), disastrous to the Christian cause far furth of Scotland. It has led to evangelistic froth which cannot stand the body of the Word at all.

I tell you that a great many of the enemies of what God has to say with massive impact to our day and generation, inside the Kirk and out of it, are in the evangelistic camp. I don't think some of these people are saved at all. The only evidence there is that they are Christians is that they like Sankey, or Redemption, or similar-style American hymns. I have found to my bitter cost that if you take these away (with their repetitive choruses which are to be sung with glazed eyes, moronic expressions, and slightly-swaying movement like primitive tribes people), they hate you like the devil. They will stand any kind of preaching provided it is dressed up in their favourite clichés. But you must not take away their ranty hymns. That is their religion. It is their god. And it is an idol which I believe must be smashed. God is calling some of us to smash it.

Twentieth Century Froth and Rigidity

There is something else before I close. So sloppy did evangelism become under the influence of the

American invasion that there was a reaction, not to the balanced devotional life of Burns, McCheyne and Bonar, but back to Wesley, or perhaps rather to a misunderstanding of him. This reacted against a mere evangelism which consumed itself in incessant activity, and which even when it did worship God could think of nothing more to talk to Him about than forgiveness and justification. It hardly knew that there was a life of sanctification in the soul of the believer which needed to be nurtured by the Word, but turned to a doctrine of holiness at once rigid and absolute which made the most fantastic claims for mere sinners. Men professed full sanctification and the blessing of a clean heart even while there was another standard in their life altogether of uncleanness and certainly uncharity.

This holiness teaching led to the most unutterable hypocrisy. I know, because I was brought up in the Salvation Army and have had a good deal to do with those who propagate this teaching. I have heard one profess there had been months in his life when he never knew himself to sin! A man's conception of sin must be very shallow, totally inadequate indeed, for him even to think like that, let alone say it. Froth and rigidity; taking things out of the Bible and making of them little verbal godlets to worship, when all the time there is the deep-sounding truth of the whole Word of God waiting for someone to unlock its mighty treasures by the Spirit—truth offering the mighty experience of death and resurrection with Jesus Christ, to change not only men's superficial ways, but their whole lives.

Complete and Contemporary

Now, all these historical aberrations, from the most profound to the most frivolous, occur when and because those who preach and practise the Christian faith do not hold together, in perfect poise or polarity, two principles. First, the whole Word—that is to say, the whole truth and nothing but the truth of the whole Bible fed to God's people in balanced diet. We must learn to be dieticians. I spend hours discussing the balanced ministry of the Word with other ministers; *e.g.* what books of the Bible, Old Testament and/or New Testament should follow one another in balanced sequence.

The second principle is that the whole Word must be saturated in the living, up-to-date grace of God by His Spirit. If we do not teach the whole Word to our people, both we and they will go astray commensurably to the extent and importance of our omissions. For example, a Christian needs the book of Proverbs and the epistle of Philemon as well as Genesis, the Psalms, Isaiah, the Gospels, Romans, Galatians, Corinthians, *etc.*

As I conclude this chapter may I say a word which will offer a hint of what is to come? The only reason why a truly regenerate and divinely called servant of God fails to be fruitful in his own day, whatever secondary reasons he hides behind, must be that he is not living in instant, tensile experience of the death/resurrection of Christ, nor is dead to all but the mighty purpose of God. All that is needed for living water to flow from one repository to another is a pipe, clean and empty, to be laid deep in the ground. There are other factors such as a good education but they are far easier to come by than this. For even if we teach the whole Word, but do so through the eyes and mind and outlook of other days, refusing to allow the living Spirit of God to make it shine in contemporary colours, then our teaching or preaching will be stale, flat and unprofitable. It will be the letter that kills, and our sermons will deserve to be the dullest things on earth. God help us!

Notes

[1] I read these words in Donald Mackinnon's Gore Memorial Lecture: *The Stripping of the Altars*, quoted from R. M. Benson, the founder of the Society of St John the Evangelist.

Chapter Four

COMMISSIONED BY GOD

You will remember that in the last chapter we discussed the danger of preachers and teachers living in other centuries than their own, and preaching in other idioms than their own. I want to return to this, not to deal generally and sweepingly with it as before, but to take up the question of the hazards you may be in in your local situation. But first let me remark that as we look back and read biblical history, we can learn not only from what was good but from what was bad in the ancients (the Bible is faithful to the faults of its men); just as when a young minister goes as assistant to some established pastor he may learn not only how to do his job, but also how *not* to do it.

Let me go back for a moment through the centuries. We know we cannot hold a candle to the unique apostles, nor to men like the Reformers. But our attitude to those outside the Bible must be categorically different from our attitude to the biblical writers, since the inspiration by which these latter wrote is categorically different to all other inspirations. The Scriptures have a perfect balance, not only between their various parts, but within these parts; there is balance at every level and in every dimension. By contrast, it is undeniable that the Reformation did more to bring forth from the Word the doctrine of justification than the doctrine of sanctification and thus fell short of that contrast. (While studying Spanish at Cambridge, one of my members, William Hunter—now lecturing at Exeter University—unearthed a most wonderful treatise on Sanctification by Louis de Leon, a sixteenth-century monk, which could give Keswick speakers a few points—allowing, of course, for medieval blemishes—and he told me he found it to be pure Augustine. When I asked him where in Augustine he found it, he replied, 'All over!')

A Shift in Emphasis

But to the Reformation. Take a copy of Calvin's commentary on Romans and put the section on the justificationary chapters (3–5) between your fingers, and then the section on the sanctificationary chapters (6–8) between other fingers, and the difference in their mere volume will indicate that Calvin exuded far more spiritual sweat on justification than on sanctification. This is no criticism; that was the need of the times. But I think the lack of exposition of the doctrine of sanctification has affected the church ever since, although that is hardly the Puritans' fault. Neither Keswick, nor so-called holiness teaching, have supplied massively or biblically enough, nor with sufficient balance, that lack. But we must not regard any man's writings with the same authority as the Scriptures. It is not only a matter of truth, but of the working balance of the truth. We will have much to say about the poise of the Spirit in the ministry of the Word, and I want you to see right away what I am driving at.

Let us telescope the intervening centuries and come right up to the influences of the last quarter of the nineteenth century and the whole of the twentieth century. Let us consider the difference between the Scottish Disruption era (the time of the Bonars, McCheyne, and Chalmers, with its crux in 1843) and that ushered in by Moody and what followed. In the earlier day, holiness or sanctification was the prevailing theme of Christian ministry, and in that context there was a wonderful evangelistic work done in the course of the ordinary parish ministry without bands, banners, or bally-hoo; whereas, a combination of the demonstrativeness of the coming of our American friend, and friends, led to the theme of justification coming so much to the fore that the whole concentration was upon bringing people to Christ, and very little on building them up in Christ. This is obvious from the missioning of the church in Scotland and Northern Ireland and the establishment of so many independent or semi-independent missions in areas where the church, alas, was not out-and-out enough in its evangelistic appeal and outreach.

Obsession with Evangelism

You may say, 'You can't build people up in Christ until you bring them to Christ.' No. But what if a complete preoccupation with bringing others to Christ overrides and ultimately neglects, then refuses, and even militates against building them up in Christ? What if we create a glut of fish and no-one to cure them? Not to speak of the dangerously superior position in which whole Christian communities find themselves when their lives are geared exclusively to mere evangelistic work. Some of the hardest nuts to crack in the Christian world are those who have been so busy evangelising that they have never allowed the Word to be turned upon them, and who therefore regard the Bible as a mere book of Gospel texts to hurl at others, or at least to bait them with. The sad decline in the quality of Christian life and witness in our country is largely due to the fact that the evangelical church has for several generations been a huge nursery, not only of infant babes but, much worse, grown-up babes. This is the same situation (or comes to the same) as when the Holy Spirit has been poured out in demonstrative effusion on the mission fields, and the church is overwhelmed by a flood of Christian babes with no-one to teach them, thus laying them open to all the carnal excesses and sectarian and heretical influences around them. I could give you a number of contemporary missionary examples of this, from New Guinea,

India, East Africa, Brazil, *etc*. For instance, someone from Brazil recently told me that,

> The rapidity of the spread of the Gospel message has resulted in many untaught Christians, who are an easy prey for cults and sects who distort God's truth; Christians need teaching by literature and Bible-teaching ministry.

Perhaps you could give instances of your own.

Is it then wrong to bring all these people to Christ? How could that be? But if a great many turn away from the truth, and ultimately from Christ, is that a good thing? Effusion of the Holy Spirit though there be (call it revival if you will), human nature is vulnerable. If our use and direction of the power and gifts of the Spirit tend in practice towards a short-sighted tactic rather than to long-term strategy (remember, in all that God does sovereignly He sees from eternity to eternity, and threads through the whole constructively and integrally), then we shall precipitate a problem that we may not have the means to solve. As a result the whole school of Christ will become one vast kindergarten, overflowing the classrooms. Nor will there be any teachers for them, because all the should-be teachers are out driving more and more infants to school. And when the teacher is away, the children play! Here then we have a school overrun, almost infested with infants, and all the monitors, guardians and teachers are out looking for more!

This inordinate desire for evangelism becomes a fever that needs to be cured. Yet it is the situation in our land today: we are suffering from an evangelistic complex, an obsession with evangelism, which at its best is too fruitless. At its worst it is sheer escape from the Christian responsibility to grow up and encourage others to grow up and make adult impacts upon the world.

This is largely because we regard the Bible as the book which contains the Gospel message. Evangelicals tend not to use the word 'contains' as liberals do who misuse it, as altering its meaning in The Westminster Confession of Faith and Shorter Catechism. However, it comes to the same in the end because although they generally hold the whole Bible to be the inspired Word of God, they far from draw upon the totality of its inspired writings. All their search is for the simple Gospel, and if they don't find the simple Gospel in its pages (some try very hard to twist and turn the Old Testament stories into it) then it is politely even reverently (but none the less actually) set aside. It becomes as much use to them, and to their hungry lambs and sheep as if they set it aside altogether with liberal contempt.

Not that they do this all the time without a twinge of conscience. Indeed many are challenged to their ire and embarrassment, and many are quite unhappy within themselves when they think about their failures to instruct and build up their giddy, gadding-about, juvenile Christians. But it is not easy in the prevailing evangelistic climate to adopt a policy of feeding the sheep on the whole Word of God, giving them a full, varied, balanced diet.

Congregations will say, 'This is not the Gospel: you do not preach the Gospel. You are not evangelical.' All because one does not preach the same hackneyed message on whatever text or passage one chooses. They have been saying that about me for years. One can safely ignore their slurs when one sees what the Word of God in breadth and depth does to people's characters so all I ever say is, 'It's in the Bible anyway. It's God's Word.' But many preachers would rather die than have people say they do not preach the Gospel. So they churn out the same old message, which leaves Christian people untouched. For the

Christians say, 'We are saved, and this is a word for the unsaved.' And they cast sidelong glances at the poor unsaved wretches who have the temerity to enter their doors, or who have been dragged there by evangelistic hunters of souls and sit cowering amongst the holy ones, getting more and more uncomfortable as they feel the eyes and attention of all in the place, including the preacher, focused on them.

How dare a minister with a balanced view of the Word of God, and with full intention of ministering it, face such a people. I know many who would rather face a firing squad than a congregation of irate Christians upon whom the Word of God has been turned. I have known far greater cruelty to the Lord's servants from such people than from nominal, unconverted church members who detest the Gospel. The devil always does a deadlier work through hardened Christians than through the unconverted, and gets far more diabolical pleasure from it, too.

A More Fruitful Way

I speak from experience. It so happens that in the beginning of my ministry our fiercely aggressive evangelistic stage lasted for eighteen months.

Incidentally, we have since had forty-nine years of solid Bible teaching of the whole Book, over and over again by means of two Sunday services, midweek Bible Studies, and by forty-eight years of Bible Study notes. Yet every new minister who comes to our town learns within weeks that we once had an evangelistic circus, which we have not had all these years. Give a dog a bad name! After eighteen months of aggressive evangelism, during which we drew large crowds, mostly of evangelistic folk from every sort of church, assembly, mission and sect, I turned the Word of God upon the Christians for the sake of the large nursery of babes we then had, many of them now grown up. Within a week, from one Sunday to another, you could not see that mission crowd for dust! Some of them have maligned me all these years for turning from the Gospel, and have even charged me with driving their mollycoddled young people into worldly pleasure halls because I ceased to provide evangelistic entertainment for them. But all I was doing was seeking to feed the lambs.

I cannot speak too strongly on this, not only from my own experience, but from that of many of my brethren in the ministry. I could take you to a church in Scotland where a gifted evangelist, burdened with the need to build up his converts, was constrained to begin teaching the Word. It began to affect his popularity, and, in the end, he gave up the attempt and went back to the weary round of evangelistic activity, to the pleasure but not the profit of his people. They could not, would not take it, and rather than lose numbers and antagonise faithful supporters, the poor chap succumbed, and has failed to strike a blow for the renewal of his congregation in our land which it was in his power to do, gifted as he was. During the years when he braved unpopularity and gave them the Word regardless, there was a harvest of missionaries and Christian workers from his congregation. But they, alas, will now have ceased.

It is, doubtless, a fine thing to be evangelistic: who is not, who deals faithfully with the Word? But it is one thing to gain converts, another to produce evangelists, missionaries, ministers—not to speak of powerful witnesses for Christ in innumerable lay fields. The church's task is not only to gain converts, but so to build them up that they are 'thrustable out'. It is the Word in its fullness and power that builds Christian character. Where people, however few, are prepared to sit under the Word in its fullness for long enough, you will find one of two things happen. They may become so roused that they will have to say to the Lord, 'Lord, what will You have me to do?' We have seen men and women well past middle life, some of them comfortably settled with grown-up families, exerting effectual witness in the lay world, being catapulted into new ministries. For example, a retired elder, a comparatively old man, from the church of which James Philip is minister, uptailed and away with his teacher wife for a two-year period of ministry to the Fair Isle. I heard him say from the pulpit before he went that it was the ministry of the Word which drove him to it. Not everyone will have to go. But all who respond to the Word will offer themselves to God

Alternatively, others will shrink back and fall into some kind of plausible sidetrack; retire gracefully—some of them perhaps not very gracefully—from the prayer meeting, and become dead wood, or even thorns in the flesh of the pastor.

Fattening the Sheep

Let us turn aside or rather stand back from all this and try to look at the whole field of pastoral ministry. Remember that 'pastoring', meaning 'pasturing', essentially has to do with feeding the flock. Let me go on to say most reverently that the task of the Christian shepherd is to fatten the sheep for the kill. In Israel that meant for sacrifice in the Temple. By 'the kill' I mean, of course, consecration. Our trouble in my own congregation is that the Lord so speedily pounces upon people whom He has sent along to be built up in the faith, that we sometimes have a hard time keeping together a working nucleus.

But to the field of pastoral ministry. It would seem that many Christian ministers accept pastorates or charges as a means of basic security—a living, as our Anglican brethren call it—and they use this as a jumping-off place for the pursuit of their pet interests in one or other of a hundred associated fields. The interest may be the application of the Gospel (or what they know, or understand, or even misunderstand of it) to politics, social service, the ecumenical movement, evangelistic work in a general inter- or non-denominational sort of way. Or it may be the running of a complex of organisations in their own church, *etc*. Many men make names for themselves in these pursuits as speakers, organisers, writers, good committee members, even as entertainers. They sustain a calling almost independent of, or that has very little to do with, the task of the pastoral ministry of feeding their sheep, from which they derive their daily bread.

Now, you may think that in this modern world I am being unreasonably hard. May I not spend a little time away from my own flock, pasturing other sheep? A good question. You answer that! I seldom accept an invitation away from my task of ministering to my own people without first refusing it. Apparently, I have something to say here that needs to be said. I hope I am saying it, and you are hearing it. What I want to say is this: Too many ministers find other things to do, either because they do not like the pastoral ministry, and find it too hard, or because it creates too many problems working with people, or because they have gone cold and dead on it and it doesn't cut much ice, and they are discouraged. Ministers must do something to justify themselves, to boost their ego and express and fulfil themselves. If they devote themselves to running large organisations, or spend their time forever on a round of vain visiting, they feel that they are doing something. Whereas if they devote themselves to the study and ministry of the Word of God, they create all sorts of problems for themselves and jangle many of their people, until their fellowships are soon in a dither of change and challenge.

Refusing to be Deflected

If we turn to something outside our congregations like Presbytery work (someone has to do it), or some other sort of work that may seem to lie easily to hand, let us not forget that we are called of God to be ministers of the Word to His people, to whom we are in fact married in the Lord. Let us also remember the prosaic fact that we are not paid by those who engage us in extra-congregational work, but by the flock whom we are neglecting to feed. This is a matter of plain ethics. It is a matter of looking for another job and neglecting to do the job we are in fact paid to do. It is exceedingly immoral, and God cannot, and will not, and does not bless those who do it. Their duty to their flock is their duty to God, and He will not bless dereliction of duty. 'Let the dead bury their dead, but you go...' and feed your flock. 'He shall feed His flock like a shepherd.' That does not mean an unending round of faithful domiciliary visits, but the feeding of their souls by the Word.

Some of my people, when I began to do this, stopped coming to church and would not allow me to speak of such things in their homes. So I wrote Bible Notes in the monthly Congregational Record and put them under their noses. That didn't make them read, but it is astonishing how much non-attenders did read. And even if it made them more anti-, well then, that is also a Christian task. We are called to be dividers of men, aren't we? (Luke 12:49–53).

I suppose the reason why we neglect this all-important duty is that we say, 'Well, I'm not making much headway amongst that stubborn lot. The Word does not seem to be making any impact upon them, and I preach and preach and preach and there is never a word of encouragement, let alone gratitude. At least what I do on the Education Committee is appreciated—or on the Inter-denominational evangelistic Committee, or in Unity, or in the Literary Association, or on the Town or Parish Council, or 'Greenpeace'—or even on UCCF!' Yes, but don't you see that a great many of these applications of the Gospel, some of them misapplications of it, are made necessary because the Christian constituency has not been vitally affected and influenced by the pastoral ministry.

The minister's job is to produce people to do all these other things. We must not do them, but produce others to do them. We must not leave the Word of God to serve tables. There are deacons, that is, other servants of God, to do these, with as great need of the fullness of the Holy Spirit (certainly of subtle, discerning grace) as ministers of the Word.

But many ministers will not see this as their task. Nor do they know, nor believe what abundant, manifold, astonishing fruit it produces in time. Anything but the ministry of the Word goes. So that when there is a drive to quicken things spiritually, someone comes away with the novel idea that we need Bible Study and Prayer and some devotional life in the congregation, and special meetings or groups in cottages or such like are arranged for prayer. To some it is a great novelty. The minister, or a leader goes round the group and asks them to discuss what they think of this passage, *etc*. What in God's holy Name are the Sunday services for, if not to feed souls on the solid Word of God—all of it. But because we will not do that, and weakly submit when a congregation says in effect that it will not stand for it, we prepare an evening service. Then, when the young upstarts say they will not come to church in the evening, we arrange for another meeting called a Youth Fellowship for them. It is like providing rounds of sweetmeats for children who refuse the solid food we have prepared for them.

One of our former associates was at one time mayor of Chippenham in Wiltshire, and he wrote to me to say what opportunities there were for Christian witness in civic and allied affairs. Of course, and it is the Christian layman's job to do them. But who will inspire them, who will drive them to them, and who will keep them evangelically sound and directed and uncorrupted in it all, but their pastor ministering the Word of God to them? We are shooting all kinds of auxiliary lines because we are failing to do our own job. One of our ministers has had an influence upon what appeared in a national newspaper (it had its aberrations too), because its editor sat Sunday by Sunday under his potent ministry. There is nothing so sorely needed in the world today as the Word of God hammered home to people's minds, hearts and wills.

The Church as a Family

By the way, one of the most injurious practices in the church psychologically, is the segregation of age-groups and sexes. I am not advising this, but one liberal man in our Presbytery decided that Sunday evening was to be 'At Home' night at the church. There would be a service for those who wanted that sort of thing. Short of course—it must be short! There would be a discussion for those who wanted that. Music and 'clubby' things for others. Dancing in the large hall for all who wanted it. He said that the young people came to him repeatedly and said that the most enjoyable thing about it all was having fathers and mothers, and even grannies and grandfathers, all the age groups and sexes together—a family.

The church of all places is meant to be a family. Not for dancing and the like, of course. Nevertheless, that man stumbled on a profound psychological principle. The only segregated activity or meeting I would ever have in church is Sunday School, and that only for younger children. Let the young find interest in the old, the old in the young, and let there be mutual care, love and service. Don't you see that all we do beyond the diets of worship and meetings for prayer and Bible Study, we do because we are failing in these? Ministers should not need to organise the church. Give the people the Word, and they should do the rest. That's what we have to give them, and there is no-one else to give it to them. We are trained and set apart for this, and if we neglect it, it doesn't matter what else we do. We fail the Christian community, then they fail, and we have to get up and do lay tasks ourselves.

The World is our Parish

I might say, as I have often said, 'What's the good of my preaching this?' Most do not believe what I say and even refuse to consider the multiple dividends of such a ministry. So they slump into a slough of sloth and discouragement, and preach without hope of anything more than making a comfortable seat for themselves, and keeping their people 'happy'. But if an increasing number of ministers began to see that this was fruitful, and did it with all their might, or rather, with all God's might and their sweat—why, the fruits of it would soon appear and would cry loud to other ministers to their great embarrassment! John Wesley said, 'the world is my parish'. Well, I can almost say the world is my parish. I don't need to

go around as he did on horseback, nor even to
travel by air around the United Kingdom to fulfil
my ministry. You see the Lord has thrust out
Christian witnesses from our poor little
congregation practically all over the world. By
staying at home and devoting all my energies to
the ministry of the Word by mouth, pen and
prayer, I can have my eyes on the Lord's work at
the ends of the earth.

The one thing I must do is keep the home fires
burning. I mean by that the fires of devotion and
prayer in the hearts of the comparatively tiny
nucleus of our people. Burning with love to God
and man, and creating an environment in which
babes and youngsters in the faith can be nurtured
and grow up to be strong, independent (in the
best sense) characters, and be driven out far and
near with the Word of God burning them up.
Thus we touch the ends of the earth from Japan
to South America, and New Zealand to North
Canada, and not only through ministers and
missionaries (full-time workers, as we call them),
for some of these can be a sore disappointment.
What great dangers there are in professionalism.
Some get bogged down with their families and
send prayer letters which have far more news
about babies and their welfare than about the

work of God. Some of the most fruitful servants of God whom I know are laymen and laywomen who, in their so-called secular vocations (they are not secular at all when Christians on fire are doing them) are touching all branches of human endeavour—politics, medicine, science, the arts, social service, *etc.*

Christian work during the last hundred years or so has tended to centre on a plethora of societies with more or less tenuous connection with the church. I mean excellent societies like YMCA, SU, even UCCF, which some have turned into their church. These have tended to draw away keen people from the church (I am not speaking personally), with the effect of making the church herself even deader than ever. In the same way, a great many less evangelical but supposedly humanitarian societies have arisen to make their own impacts for good upon the community and upon the nation as a whole, because the church was making little or no impact.

We all accept that the remedy for a church that was going dead towards the end of the nineteenth century was not to run away from it and start new substitutes. Can we not, therefore, see that the remedy for the church's effeteness today is not to give up hope of the pastoral ministry and run into something else. There is no remedy in school teaching, local government, becoming deputation secretaries to missionary societies, freelance evangelists, or any of a host of humanitarian or social service jobs—not to speak of far less evangelical things than these. The remedy for all who are called to this highest of all earthly tasks is to concentrate on it with all their might, or as we said before, with all God's might, patience and faithfulness, and see what vital impacts that will make upon the people of God. Upsetting impacts some of them will be, but we will find that we make our mark upon others and upon our day and generation, although we may be dead long before they recognise it. That does not matter, the prize-giving is 'Upstairs'.

There is no greater or better way to make impact than by sounding forth the Word of God and bringing people under its life-changing and character-transforming power. The reverberations of such a ministry extend further and further, and the ramifications of its influence spread farther abroad than we ever dreamt of—and all without thought on our part or attempt at publicity, self-aggrandisement or self-justification.

This is all part of my same theme. If we don't do our job, the most important job in the world, of providing salt to save our society from corruption, and light for Gospel witness to gather the church, then not only we, but all other ministers will have to attend to a thousand-and-one worse ways of trying to make impacts on our society. They will often have to do so in carnal strength, like the blind leading the blind. It is not too much to say that not only the church, but the world, is dying for lack of the infinitely manifold fruits of the ministry of the Word of God.

Now, all the time I am speaking, you will be aware, if you are with me at all, that I am begging many questions. But I assure you there are answers to them. Do get my point which is, that if the hope of the world is Christ, it is Christ in all the Scriptures, and that hope can only be fulfilled by men pouring out the riches of Christ's saving grace upon the Lord's people through the Scriptures.

The Call

I am pretty sure that some of you are saying, 'I know many chaps who are trying to do this, and it doesn't have all that effect.' Well, has it got

something to do with the personality of the one
who ministers? I am sure that the personality of
the one who ministers is not unimportant. Nor
do I believe that God calls us to be timid little
mice, or ineffectual little 'yes-men' in the
ministry. But this I know: that, as God can use
those with no more than turnips for heads and
make them exude the sweetest and most
nourishing spiritual juices to their people, so He
can take the most frightened and frightening little
bookworms—boring little creatures who bore
into books all the week and bore their heads into
manuscripts on Sundays so that they bore all the
poor people who are bored enough to put up with
them—and can make them both mighty and
courageous. Like Jeremiah, for instance. God does
not call us to this gigantic task to be flops.
Remember, when the Chaldeans came to
Jerusalem in 586 BC they took poor fruitless
Jeremiah, whom the Jews would not listen to for
a moment with any intent, and the Chaldeans
said to him (while busy slaughtering most of the
Jews, and carrying the best of them to Babylon),
'What would you like to do, Jeremiah? Just tell
us, and we will do it. Anything you like!' These
pagans appreciated him, even if the Jews did not.

The key is the Call. If you are not absolutely sure, or cannot come soon to absolute assurance that God has laid His hand upon you for this work—flee it. One of our professors used to say (you will have heard this old chestnut, but it speaks profound truth), 'No-one should be a minister if he can be anything else in the world.' Alas, many have become ministers who should not, and some who should have tried in weak frustration to do anything and everything else in the world because it was easier. If some want to be politicians, or school teachers, or social workers, or servants of local government, what help will a minister's collar be to them, or 'Reverend' before their name? Some think the minister's collar is not much help to a minister, or 'Reverend' either. 'Reverend', indeed. Who? Me? You? I know we are called to be God's servants but what help do trappings lend us? They are only for those who don't have the real thing to bolster them up. Those who are real just tolerate them.

Don't be a minister if you can help it. It is the worst job in the world. But it is also the best. I am convinced that in the present state of the church, only a comparatively small proportion of those who go forward to the ministry are really called of God. Indeed, going back through the years of my ministry, of the scores whom I have seen go into the ministry of various denominations, and other associated ministries, some I would not now approve for it at all. Why not? What is wrong? Some of them should not be in it. Some should, but they've got the wrong wife. Others have allowed the right wife to take a dominant place. Some are lazy. Others are too absorbed in the ceaseless round of congregational life. Some are plain 'feart' as we say in Scotland; afraid of repercussions within the congregation if they are fully faithful, for they think that anything that upsets the congregational life, especially the good givers and attenders, must be wrong. I simply do not know how they square that with our Lord upsetting the tables in the temple precincts. Yet others think they are too poor and small to be of any use.

Too many are worldly enough to think in terms of numbers and statistics, forgetting that there was only one Christ, three special disciples, twelve in all—and one of these a devil. One of the things the Bible teaches us is the value of one man. Moody said that, didn't he? 'The world has not yet seen what God can do with a man utterly yielded to Him.' In a sense, dear D. L. Moody was wrong, for the world had seen uniquely in Christ what God could do with a Man utterly yielded to Him, as the world has seen in many others, including Moody himself. Remember that the mighty effect of high explosives in quarries begins with boring tiny, long holes into rocks, and laying charges of terrific potential in them.

Make sure you are called to the ministry, because the world gets worse and worse, and if ever there was a day when an evangelical minister could become a conventional member of society and fulfil a merely social role or occupy an official status, it is not today. In which land is the church not in a real missionary situation as pilgrims and strangers in an alien, enslaved world? Even places with a rich evangelical heritage can take nothing for granted. When the superficially evangelistic community exhausts the solid biblical capital it has inherited from its forefathers, what is there to fall back upon? There is more likelihood that it will become increasingly worldly in ostensible attempts to maintain communication with the lost world than that it will be willing to be led back to a solid biblical diet by ministers called of God to give it what it needs and not what it wants. You need to be called of God to stick out from a complacent, alien community like a sore thumb. Nor will you need to try to stick out. Just be faithful, and God will arrange it, and you will be the talk of the community, however self-effacing you try to be.

Now, don't think I am merely voicing my own thoughts. I am drawing from the experience of not a few throughout our land. I know ministers who are so heartbroken by the refusal of professing Christian folk to be fed on a solid diet of the Word of God that they would give up the whole thing if they had not been arrested by God for the task. But like Martin Luther they can do no other.

The Right Place

Equally, we must be in our God-appointed place in the ministry. This is vitally important. A minister may be authentically called of God, and may have had abundant evidence in one place that God was there, but due to circumstances, personal or otherwise, a move to another place is made and the ministry goes dead. The new congregation is out of the Lord's will. Alas, all the plausible excuses in the world—the wishes of a spouse, the educational needs of a family, the difficulties of office-bearers and members, *etc.*, will not justify a move out of God's will.

I recall an old lady, very prominent in evangelical circles, coming to me about one of my local fellow ministers whose name had been a household word in the Presbyterian Church in both Scotland and England, asking if I could help him. He had confessed to her that since he left the charge in which God had wonderfully blessed him, he had known himself to be a failure in God's sight—despite having been in several so-called 'important' charges since (he had left because there was trouble—he literally ran away from it). I called on him in hospital to see if he would open up to me, but rather bitterly and sarcastically he said he was sure I had better things to do than visit him, he had plenty of visitors anyway. He died a little later, of two kinds of heart trouble.

If you are called of God, you are not your own, and you are certainly not your wife's, nor your children's, nor even your congregation's. Keep close to God, there is no substitute for that. Others may give you advice, but unless they are in the same position of waiting in holy fear before the God of all the earth, the God of their calling, their advice is not worth having. Don't assume that God will tell another what you should do. It does happen, but in special circumstances. Of course, God tells a man and his wife (if they are married in the Lord) the same things. Otherwise, God alone may be listened to.

Dying to Live

Another thing: to minister fruitfully (and God does not call us to anything else) we must minister as those who have died. This is really the same point as the last, but it has total ramifications in the life. It is only out of a life that is dead not only to sin (obvious) but to self in all its various and subtle aspects, that God will bring resurrection to others. Death works in us, but life in others (2 Cor. 4:12). That is the profoundest and most practical principle in the Bible. Every time we essay to minister there must be a new death. 'Deaths oft...I die daily,' said Paul. It is the glorious agony of those who are used of God amidst the oppositions of the world, the church, and certainly the devil, that we are ever dying men and women.

When I first saw this, it was the most comforting light I think I had ever seen. For, after a year and a half of eye and ear-catching ministry that hit the headlines, at divine behest I turned to minister the Word to Christians and the work began to dwindle as far as numbers were concerned. It has been dwindling ever since, until for many years now we have seemed to be on our last legs, and all and sundry have been prophesying our end. We have worked with increasingly smaller numbers. While we have a congregation of active and fruitful servants of God scattered about the earth who would fill our ample church several times over if they were all in one place at one time (they will never be, on earth), the handful of people we are working with at one time is so small that people who come into our midst from afar say, 'Is this all?' A couple from Canada once almost left our church before the service when they saw how few were present. This couldn't be the place they had heard about! After the service went on a little they thought perhaps it was!

You can see what a death this is to die to those who think you are nothing if not popular. If we are not prepared to suffer (and suffering is not fun nor is it meant to be fun), we shall not reign. The two belong together, as Peter says over and over again in his first epistle. Hurt and fruit, death and life, sorrow and joy. They belong together, as manure belongs to a fruitful garden.

Prayer

One other thing: prayer. We must challenge our people to pray for the ministry, and must see to it that however we meet, and whatever you call it, there is a backing, a support, a power-house of prayer behind our ministries. You may go into a new place on the prayer support of Christian friends, or your home church, as young ministers do, but you must early seek to establish the connection in your people's minds between your living ministry and their prayers, no matter how painfully you start. I know one struggling place where scarcely any one has ever attended the prayer meeting except the minister and his wife, but they still carry on and hope. That's the spirit. Happy the people (however tiny the nucleus) who begin to see, or can be made to see, that they have the makings of the ministry, if not the minister, in their own hands by prayer. It was an old lady between 80 and 90 years of age who prayed me, all unknown, into my place and then prayed me into the forefront of the battle with me resisting, in terror, a good part of the way until I caught the thrill of heavenly warfare.

If you are going into the ministry for a comfortable seat, and to fulfil yourself, rear a happy family, gather a happy congregation around you and end up with a nice plaque on the church wall for your 'gracious ministry', but nothing more, then you will long since have ceased to listen to me. But maybe you have heard. If so, then my breath and the searchings of my own heart and mind will not have been in vain.

Chapter Five

WALKING THE TIGHTROPE

You may think that I have not dealt with my subject, the Ministry, as it needs to be dealt with, but what I have to say is something not easy to express. In a sense, it is something which can only be expressed by the dynamic of the Holy Spirit. As fallen creatures in a fallen world presently lying under the power of the evil one, and ourselves only in process of perfection, the God-honouring and fruitful minister walks a tightrope; and, if you will allow me to say it reverently (after all, Jesus used shocking figures), it is a tightrope of the Spirit. A ridiculous figure? Certainly a difficult one to develop and apply. For one thing, as far as the ministry of the Word is concerned, it involves the balance between the past and the present. It also involves the balance of being 'in this world', the world in which impacts are to be made, and yet 'not of it'.

Finding the Balance

We must not live in the world of books, but in the world of real people. Yet, all that is worth saying to them of lasting value comes from books. But it is all summed up in One who was a real person; and the end is never propositions, theories, precepts, doctrines, but a certain kind of flesh and blood. The Word became flesh to be a real person in you and me for ever. God will never cease to be Man. He is a Man for ever. The hope is not in animality of any level or order, not in angelality of any rank or order, but in Man, the crown of creation. The tightrope of the Spirit is that fine tension on which communication is established and maintained between the Man Christ Jesus and human sinners whom He came to save. And the danger which the tightrope walker, the minister of the Word, is in is that of falling headlong and disastrously to the one side into the archaic past or, equally disastrously, to the other side into the vain present and becoming lost in aimless contemporaneousness, in futile 'with-it'-ness, of being in the world and so 'of it' that no impacts are made upon it at all.

This poise requires that we know Christ and His Word, and understand Him in His Word to be all sufficient, and to be the final, absolute Word to the world. It also requires that we live in our own day, and do not cut ourselves off from what others are thinking, saying and doing in our day—from the means of communication. We must know what is going on in the world. We certainly haven't time to know it all. It is not all significant, anyway, and a lot of it is inanely repetitive and we certainly haven't time for all the detail. We must know what the newspapers are saying (some of them), what radio and television are up to, what the local council is saying, what the people are doing with their leisure time, and what sort of clandestine activities go on in our areas under cover of night. We must know about the dens of wickedness, in the west end as well as in the east end of towns and what wicked things are done amongst rural people. We must know what the intellectuals are saying, or are trying to say in books, plays and articles. We must know the trends in general, and what the Word has to say to them, and how far the contemporary church has failed to say the truth. We must know, not least, what the common people are saying and doing; and certainly, without any unhealthy preoccupation, we must know what the drab, wild youngsters are up to. We will have some understanding of the trends in science, philosophy, education. We must be under no illusions regarding the secularisation of society and the consequent almost total ignorance among children of the Christian faith and spiritual values. And we will certainly be very much aware of the abandonment of morality in the nation, due to the fact that the Word of God on the lips of the clergy has lost practically all its moral and spiritual authority.

No Fear of God

There is no fear of God before men's eyes today. And the church is fairly and squarely to blame. If people feared God, the perverse so-called intellectuals, the aimless 'dirt-boys', whether playwrights, novelists or dispensers of high-falutin' satire, would never dare to be as arrogantly insolent, as mercilessly contemptuous of anything holy, pure, good and true, as they are.

Some time ago an academic on the Scottish BBC Council, where standards of decency and of religious broadcasting used to be higher than in England (I don't know about television elsewhere), tackled the Director-General of the BBC on the filth on television, and he reported that the men in London were arrogantly contemptuous of his criticism. This must necessarily shock us, but it must not appal us. We know our Bibles. The like has been known before, many times, although not in present-day colours. We will look back to the wickedness of the generation before the flood and see Noah industriously doing two things: building a boat of salvation, and preaching righteousness to a generation about to be swept away.

What was the point of preaching righteousness to them? Wasn't it a waste of time? No. When Jesus preached to the spirits in prison between His mortal death and resurrection, it was very likely to the spirits who led astray that race of Noah's day. Christ proclaimed judgement on them. He did not evangelise them. They were beyond that (look at the Greek and see). May He not also have had a look at the damned antediluvians and said to them, 'You have no excuse. Noah preached to you for a hundred years and more before the flood, warning you what your end would be.'

As we look out, then, upon the wickedness of the day, we will not panic, or fear. Nor will we be complacent. We will seek to see it through the eyes of the mighty saints of old who faced such evils, and we will seek their spirit that we may see our place in the world of contemporary wickedness and evil in absolutely up-to-date terms. That is to say, we will know what to do about it.

We will see how Samuel dealt with the nation of Israel who had gone astray under a careless priesthood (1 Sam. chs 4, 7). We will see Israel and Judah in Isaiah's day; Judah a hundred years later on in Jeremiah's day, when he said the human heart was incurably wicked. We will look at the high-bred idolatry of the Athens of Paul's day and the corruption of the church of Martin Luther's day. And we will see that no craven panic made them run with palliative poultices of moralistic or sociological orders to cure deadly cancers, nor with sweetly perfumed unguents to heal deep-seated leprosies. They knew God and His Word, and they knew by the Spirit of God what the Word was for that hour. They knew how it should be stated—thundered, in fact, remembering that thunder is not always deafeningly loud, but can rumble ominously all the same. They simply applied God's Word to their day, and from all that God had said to former generations (they were for ever harking back to Israel in Egypt and in the wilderness), they were able to pick out the relevant Word for their day.

Nor was it all judgement, although that is the Word for days of wickedness. For the judgement passages in the prophetic writings are continually interspersed with passages of pure comfort to the faithful, and with encouragement to them to endure in hope in the evil day. For whatever the evil day may bring to the world in general, only they who trust in the Lord have hope.

Knowing your Bible

By the way, I wonder how well you know your Bibles? I don't mean the detail, so that there isn't an obscure name in the Old Testament you cannot locate, but how able are you to sweep through the Old Testament and sum up its history in a few meaningful strokes of intelligent delineation, leading to Christ?

Many ministers do not use what they know. I am astonished at how much divinity students know, yet how little ministers give to their flocks.

For example, take Abram brought out of the Persian Gulf to Canaan and his grandson Israel brought to Egypt with a family. Twelve tribes were at last brought from Egypt's slavery to a new birth as a nation to serve God's purposes on the 'death/resurrection' night and morning of the Passover. They were brought into the wilderness, then into the Promised Land, and made glorious under David and Solomon. When the seeds of sin in the lives of these great kings led to the ruin of the nation by adultery, natural and spiritual (called idolatry), they were set aside as a nation (Isa. chs 6–10). God then concentrated His hope in a remnant, which having been retrieved from Babylon's purging fires, He preserved, as they clung to the rock of Zion in subjection and penury for five hundred years. By then the royal blood of David's line was reduced to that of a poor peasant maid, and the village carpenter. Do not forget that Joseph the joiner was very likely the rightful king of Israel in his day, as his descent from Solomon and David makes plain; see Matthew 1 and Luke 3. The Hope of the world, who was to come of Israel, was born of this maid, Mary, and was sheltered by that man, Joseph. And all this because of God's faithful judgements on His own people.

Note that sweep, and the meaning of that sweep. The story begins with a man, Abram, and rises to a nation, and descends again to a remnant, and thence to a Man. Think of it again: from a man, to a nation, to a strange hidden kingdom of innumerable remnants (the hidden Kingdom, the *ecclesia*, the 'called-out ones' of every generation). The new Kingdom is established through a Man who is Head of a new race, a race mysteriously born before the unseeing eyes of the world. This race grows in grace and power where Christians are being nurtured and matured by the Word through the Spirit. A Kingdom amasses an inconceivable concourse in heaven until the great day of the outshining and outshowing of its glory, when the King comes with His Kingdom of holy priests to establish righteousness and holiness in heaven and earth.

What an amazing conception! How could any of us be put off balance in any day, whatever it held or threatened, if we knew that that was what we were engaged in furthering. Some ministers I know, for light relief from the burden of holy work, read complicated novels full of tangles and twists and intriguing and unexpected cleverness. But not in their wildest dreams (or their favourite authors' wildest dreams) have they come across

anything so exciting, fabulous, fantastic as this
that God has done and is doing. Truth is stranger
than fiction. It is so devastatingly simple and yet
so appallingly difficult and complex. Yet it makes
sense, and is the only thing that properly makes
sense in our crazy world.

People who are too easily intimidated by the
wickedness of any one generation and who panic
over things which go wrong, are living so near
their own day that they have lost the message of
the ages which is full of such seeming disasters. It
is they who run with their poultices and eyewash
to meet the needs of the hour instead of abiding
by the radical measures of the Word of God
which gets down to the elements of the case. It is
like trying to purify foul water at the tap, instead
of at the reservoir or the poisoned stream. There
is an application of the Word of God for even the
most urgent contemporary situations, but if we
get all hot and bothered about it, and myopically
concentrate all our ministry on that, for ever
moaning from our pulpits about the evils of the
day, what are the hungry sheep going to feed
upon the while? The devil is a master of sidetrack.

The Church in the World

If you were a layman, say a Member of Parliament, or a member of your urban or rural council, then as an individual lay Christian, and as a righteous person serving your day and generation for Christ's sake, you ought to take such matters up and do all you can about them. Cyril Black did this for many years at Westminster (although, remember what I said about the nineteenth-century social reformers). But as a minister you cannot turn aside to deal with political or sociological questions. Who is going to perform your task of feeding the sheep if you do? What of the Kingdom of God? If all the ministers in one generation essayed the task of making our human conditions better, more decent and worthy so only a few were added to Christ, and those who were added were left as undernourished starvelings because the ministers were at the political and sociological front, what would happen to that generation's representation in the heavenly repository? If for fifty years, or even less, few saints were added to the heavenly waiting-rooms, and those who were, were all babes, what would the Lord do? His perfect plan for all the ages would be put out, and the church would never be the perfect whole He has conceived it should be.

Although in itself it is a good thing, a little temporary alleviation of the conditions of men on the earth is as nothing compared with the task of building a house of God of human, living stones, and a Kingdom of redeemed humanity come to Christly maturity. Where is the reign of God in any generation? It is in the church. The believers are the children of the Kingdom, and God's ministers, or shepherds, are called to gather the flock, feed them and prepare them for their translation to the heavenly waiting-place, until the Kingdom comes in fullness. When you think of the world, think, I bid you, that as hell is filling up, so is heaven. The growing population of the ungodly in any generation is as nothing before the concourse of saints who await the Great Day.

This is not said to make us complacent about the evil. If we are, we must cease to be, and have a look into the belly of hell, and then draw back in terror, seeking to draw others back from it in equal terror, dragging them out of the fire. But the evil is so rampant and manifest and impudent that I do not think that any God-called ministers can be complacent today; they are much more likely to be in despair. But we must not be so.

Our job is to add to the concourse that is waiting in heaven, and not merely add evangelistically to its nurseries (*cf.* 1 Cor. 3:10–15), but to the number of those who, because they have bravely and willingly suffered with Christ and for Christ on earth, shall reign with Him aloft.

Therefore, ministers of the Word in the 1990s, or 1890s, or 1590s, or 2090s, must do the very same thing, although it will have a unique contemporary slant and application suited peculiarly to its own day as to no other. They will preach the whole Word with continual application to those, however few they may be, who hear its message and its timely import. They will do this undeviatingly, undistractedly and undeterredly (remember Noah's boat and his words of warning; remember Isaiah's and Jeremiah's words of warning to the nation, and their comfort to the faithful). Whatever any generation may have to see and endure, preachers of the Word of God will be continually busy fitting the saints for the power and glory. That is a perennially valid and authentic work which neither time, nor the devil, nor hell can undo. Such preachers will have their minds fully on their work of gathering and upbuilding the church. Yet they will live with their eyes opened wide upon every significant event of their day, of which what is happening in and to the church is always the most significant. After all, that is the only thing which is going to last—except hell.

They will take the sharp sword of the Word of God, as it applies to the wicked things of their day, and drive that sword home to the dividing asunder of things soulish from things spiritual, and to the exposure, not only of wickedness where it lies and lurks, but of what underlies it. I refer not only to the human agents of the devil but also to the demonic squadrons and diabolical legions that take their disorderly orders from the devil himself. Preachers will never be sidetracked by evil. They will never let the devil out of their sight; yet they will not take their mind off what the Spirit is saying and doing through them. It is because they are bent upon doing the Spirit's behest that they must keep 'shooing' the devil away. They allow themselves to be distracted temporarily only that they be not distracted permanently.

A Glorious Prospect

There is a difference between God's programme for His Kingdom, and that misconceived by a

misunderstanding church and world. It is that
God does not hope to build a Kingdom in one
generation in the hope that fallen sinners of the
next generation will meekly follow in their
fathers' footsteps. It is the exact opposite. Good
fathers produce bad sons. Don't ask me why. See
Manasseh, the son of Hezekiah, and Jehoiakim
and Zedekiah, the sons of Josiah who was the
godliest king of all Judah and Israel.

God pins His hope on the remnant in every
age who live in Messianic hope and power. He
looks to them massing in heaven with growing
excitement (if we may use such an
anthropomorphic word of the Almighty), until at
last their number being complete, the mass of the
heavenly host grows so great, and becomes so
clamant for the vindication of the martyr saints,
that with divine consent they break out, under
the leadership of their divine Lord and overrun
and overflow the whole creation. Dramatic, isn't
it?

As soon as the hope of Israel's national reunion
and restoration to glory and power faded in
Isaiah's and Jeremiah's day, God's prophets
turned under divine direction to the hope of a
remnant in whose hearts the Law would be
written by the Spirit. Thus alongside the

denunciations and warnings they thundered out there came forth sweet words of comfort for the faithful. Hope indeed!

It is not so much that hope was seen in the light of the coming judgement, but the judgement was seen in the great light of the coming hope which could not fade. It was because the hope was sure (it was founded on the rock of Zion) that the judgement could be voiced roundly without fear that the Lord's dear people would misunderstand, panic, and become demoralised. Their hope was not set on a little temporary worldly respite but on Christ the solid Rock, all other ground being sinking sand. The hope then could emerge only from the judgement. The rainbow could shine only on the cloud. The new growth could rise only from the rotting remains of last season's seed and corms and tubers. The pure gold could appear only from the scalding dross in the crucible.

To put it otherwise and more simply: a shepherd is no mere warder-off of wild beasts. To save the sheep from wild beasts and all other dangers is not to feed them; and if they are not fed, what matters whether they are safe or not? What is the good of being saved to starve? We must be saved in health and strength, unto maturity and power to reign with Christ in His Kingdom. And for that we must be fed. Every temptation to be sidetracked from the task of eternity which is the task of the hour—your hour—must be seen in relation to the finished product. What is the end of what you are doing? The God-appointed end?

The Miracle of Grace

I began, you may remember, by saying that the only way to engage in God-honouring and fruitful service in any day was to walk the tightrope of the Spirit, that is, the tightrope of a Spirit-filled and Spirit-inspired ministry of the Word of truth. But you may not like the metaphor. Well, I will tell you why I use it. It is a kind of miracle that any one should walk on a thin line of rope with all that unsubstantial air around him. It almost defies the laws of nature. A frail fallen sinner is hardly fit for so skilled an exploit. It is only by superb balance that the tightrope walker is preserved from instant destruction. Nor does it matter which side he falls on. His only safety is in perfect balance.

It is like that with the minister in the world. 'The whole world lieth in the evil one'; and it is nothing short of a miracle when any one becomes a saint of God; it is a supernatural work. God has enabled us to excel and surpass ourselves and become something greater than our fallen selves—real people. And it is all the greater miracle that the servant of God becomes anything at all on account of the madness of the foe. It is only as we see it as a miracle of the grace of God that we are used to do anything for Him that it is likely to happen.

If we think it is going to be easy, if we think it is going to be natural—others fail but wait till we get a start, we will show them! If we think too easily that we will override the dangers that have got better ministers than we down, then we are certainly going to collapse. It matters not whether we collapse on the side of sound deadness, or on the side of activists beating the air. We collapse and whatever the world may say about it, since we may collapse on to a very honoured position, on to a net, forsooth, or on to some luxurious carpet of deepest pile, we are off the tightrope where the Spirit alone can keep us poised to do a fruitful work for God.

Losing your Balance

There are two dangers, and we are attacked from two points of view. One, that of being so preoccupied with soundness in the truth, with doctrines, formulations, propositions and principles, that we go all academic and dead. (Now, surely no-one will think that I am anti-academic. Come and see how hard I work at scholarship, although I will never be a scholar, and you will soon get that idea out of your head.)

The other danger is that we go all activist, constantly running round in fruitless circles, constantly stirring the pot of emotionalism to boiling point, equating the presence and the working of the Spirit with noise, clatter, chatter, laughter and tears, clapping of hands and wringing of hands, *etc.*

In practice it is impossible—I say impossible—for us to preserve the perfect balance of soundness, and withal the spiritual vitality essential to a living ministry without the poise that comes from the Spirit alone. There is much soundness from which, alas, the Spirit has departed, and soundness soon then becomes *rigor mortis.* The Spirit departs because the Word must become flesh to confront and challenge and penetrate the minds and hearts, the consciences and wills of other flesh. Some will give any bribe to God to save them becoming powerhouses of the Holy Ghost, which they ought to become supremely in preaching. The Word comes alive in flesh and blood; that is why a life can challenge sometimes without words—although the life that does challenge without words will never be a life lived without judicious, timely, gracious and searching words.

On the other hand, because the Word can only be ministered effectually by the Spirit inspiring human flesh that is not to say that every spirit is the Holy Spirit. The difference between the Holy Spirit and other spirits is the difference between the tightrope, a thin line of real substantiality, and the unsubstantial air that allows us to be gravitated off the tightrope. The devil is not so much concerned with our destruction as with getting us off that tightrope before we achieve anything by way of the Word reaching decisively into our people's minds and hearts. There are many spirits, and we must try them, as John tells us, by bringing them to the touchstone of the full truth of Jesus Christ, a truth which comes only to fruition and full outshining in the transformation of human character. Partial truth will not transform human character until it shines and glows and flames (transfiguration).

True truth, as far as it goes, which allows carnal, fallen Adamic preachers of an alien spirit to apply a partial Christ to the old Adam (like giving an old photograph a new face, an old man a new pair of legs, or dressing up an old doll in new supposedly Christian clothes) will not do. It is the eternally contemporary Spirit of Jesus Christ from of old, yet ever new, who comes to take the old things of the Word of God and makes them shine in instant light, giving illumination, often painfully, to all who are in the house, and showing up everything good and bad which is within that house. It is the eternally contemporary Spirit of Christ who takes the hidden things of the Spirit, scarcely known to us or understood by us, and makes them clear and apparent in the context of the most practical living. He makes them touch everyday things. He speaks authoritative words on all sorts of subjects—moral, religious, personal, domestic, communal.

Keeping your Balance

This masterly poise comes only by the instant Spirit of Jesus Christ working in the lives of His chosen ones as they allow Him unrestricted sway. Yet it involves a tremendous training and discipline, doubtless with long courses of intellectual training in biblical truth, like Moses' forty years in Midian, Jesus' thirty years in Nazareth, Paul's years in Arabia. We are so eager, we want a short training and a long ministry. Jesus had thirty years' training and three years' ministry. But whether the training be long or short, it must at all events be thorough. For fruitful, spiritual poise a vital, personal contact is involved (almost an electrification) with decisive touchstones. Here are some of them.

Know Christ

Firstly, you must know Christ as Person to person (*cf.* the lamp of faith in 2 Pet. 1:19 with the daystar arising in believers' hearts by the coming of Christ). Is Christ in you a mere lamp of faith, or a sun blazing with glory? Has Christ grown up in you, so that there is far more of Christ in you than the remnants of old Adam? You must not only believe on Him or into Him, you must know Him as the most authoritative Person in your life.

Be sure of your call

Secondly, you must know or be seeking decisive assurance that you are called by Him to minister the Word; and you must eventually, before you begin, be so certain of this that you would die at the stake for your knowledge.

Wait for His will

Thirdly, you must be willing to await His will. Some of the most fruitful ministers I know in Scotland have had to wait years for their God-given appointments. And I might add that some have to wait for years in what I call a preparatory ministry, which is often more for their own personal good than for what an unwilling evangelistic people bargained for. You must be sure that you are in the right place. Only one thing kept me in my pulpit when all hell was let loose against me: it was the knowledge that God put me there, and there I had to stay until God took me out. I have hurled this more than once at my enemies with, I assure you, devastating effect!

Die to yourself

Fourthly—and most important of all—in your personal, intimate, up-to-date knowledge of Christ, secure in His calling, anchored, rooted to your right place, you must in fact die at the stake to all you are in yourself, bad and good. Do not forget that while Jesus died with all our badness to take it away, He had to die to all the good He could have been and could have done in a long earthly life, in order that He might die with our badness. It is this, I am sure, that most, even perhaps the best equipped ministers, find themselves not brave enough to rise to, or rather to get down to. We must die a total death to self ('be yielding yourselves unto God' in Romans 6:13 is not 'reckoning yourselves dead indeed unto sin', but surrendering your Christ-born life to Him for His will). Paul comes back to this in chapter 12, where he says we are to hand ourselves over to God like a defeated soldier surrendering arms—a living sacrifice. Far harder to live for Him a living death than to die for Him a death which is an escape or exodus.

If you ask why I rub this in, and make it seem so painfully hard, I answer, because I cannot make it sound too hard. It is far worse to do than you may have dreamed of. Many young ministers have come to me a year or two after they have been out in the ministry, having sought to put what they have learned into practice, and they have had a new respect for the hard things they were taught but took with a pinch of salt. This is a radical business. It is literally (no metaphor) a matter of life and death.

Let us put it in electrical terms. You have to die a total death to self to let the current of God's power through to others. There is an old story about the early days of broadcasting. It was said to concern the very first Christmas broadcast of King George V, when a vital wire in Buckingham Palace was found to be broken and there was no time for the engineer to do anything but hold the two ends together in his burning hands to let the current, and the king's message, pass through. (There is also a version of this which says that vital current passed through the dead body of a man who gave his life to preserve communications in war.) How far this accords with electrical fact is not my concern but I do know to my very great, sore, deadly, heartbreaking, agonising cost, that the Word will never come through someone living. That person must be dead. (If you knew what deaths I have had to die to be here at all!) Preachers must be negative to the positive charge of God. There must be no carnal resistance in them to the Word they declare. In fact, if we are not one hundred per cent 'with it', that is, with God in what He is doing through us, we are beating the air, wasting our breath, working for mere wages, with no product whatsoever for our pains.

Don't go it alone

Fifthly, no-one as an individual Christian can do this. The old Latin tag that there is no salvation outside the church is never so true as in this connection. As those who are saved are added to the church, certainly no-one is or can be saved, except through the ministry (using the word in its total sense) of the church. I believe no-one ever does any good for God or for Christ's sake anywhere, without other Christians at some time and in some place having had a part in it. The church is one in her work. None of us works on our own.

Someone picks up a scrap of paper from a tract or Testament in the wilderness and is saved. This is probably never a direct act of the Spirit. Someone put it there, even if inadvertently. Either the prayerful intent, or some other Christian in mutual prayer fellowship, known or unknown, held the wires of God's communication together. The Spirit sent Philip from Samaria to Gaza, and found the eunuch hurrying home in his Rolls Bentley. Who was behind it? It was maybe the prayer fellowship of the church in Samaria, who to their own dismay found that they had prayed their leader away to found the Christian church in Ethiopia. 'Come over into Macedonia and help us.' Was the 'man of Macedonia' an angel? Even so, he must have been someone's angel. Some praying soul or souls was or were crying for a Paul to cross the Aegean Sea.

I am not saying that the Spirit never acts directly through the Word alone (although I could well believe it, and would like to believe it). But it is not normally His way. God respects humanity, especially the new humanity He has created in Jesus Christ, and seeks no other than His church to do His work. And by the church I mean the vital, loving fellowship of those who are bound together in effectual bonds of prayer between pray-ers and preachers—not to say livers of the Word—who are Christ's several ministers of salvation to the world. He has no other, and seeks no other. When Jesus ascended, He left eleven men to do His work and, promising them

His Spirit, left them, inflamed by the Spirit, to do it. He had no other plans.

But I am straying. The point is that none of us can preach effectually on our own. We must be sent out by the church, by the praying church, whatever nondescript company of Christians that may be. I think I said before that both missionaries and ministers should have their home church behind them. They should send them out. If they feel, alas, that they are out on a limb, all on their own, as many missionaries feel, they may well question their calling—unless they can find help and guidance to relate themselves to some group somewhere who are prepared to own them, and who will care for them and be prepared to thrust them forth into the battle. I grant that ministers may not find such a group until they find themselves in their first charge, and discover that their people, all unknown to them, had been fishing in all waters for them, until up they came, when both fish and fisher with delight said, 'Hello, I was looking for you!'

Summary

Let us go over the points again. We must know Christ. We must be called by Him, none other, to

His service. We must know at any time where He wishes us to serve. We must die to all sin and self, and indeed, to all good and ill. And we must know ourselves to be part of the sending and praying church which is constantly engaged in gathering the loose ends of the communicating currents of God's Spirit and holding the right lines together, not getting them crossed, holding them together with burning hands and hearts of prayer, costly prayer. And lastly, we must know and understand that the vital, worshipping, serving church of Jesus Christ is ever a remnant, of a remnant, of a remnant of the so-called church. Yet, like Jesus and Paul and all the Old Testament prophets we must never, until the last desperate agonising moment, perpetrate schism, and take ourselves out of a nominal or backsliding church. (Thrown out you may be, that is different.) Judas partook of the Lord's Supper and Jesus suffered him to do so. Remember what Paul predicted and what doubtless came to pass in Ephesus after his last farewell with the elders, that enemies not only from without but from within would arise. Read Paul's letters to Timothy, and elsewhere, and you will find in the New Testament that all the power of the enemy will be focused upon nominal and backsliding Christians in order to ruin and render ineffectual Christ's church. We must never take fright and run away into some Adullam's cave of divisive security. There is no security there. Schismatics all die if they do not return to the fold.

Many Christian societies and associations, missionary societies, indeed, are dying today, but the ancient church will not die. I am not speaking of denominations as such, but of the true church of Christ standing upon the whole Word of God and upon the vital witness, imperfect though it may be, of the contemporary branch of the church of the Christian ages. The church cannot die. Do not desert what appears to you to be a sinking ship. Jesus is in her, although He may seem to you to be asleep—not much wonder with the exertions of trying to keep her awake! Rouse Him, and He will yet save her. If the Roman Catholics ever gave us a red face, would it embarrass you?

One of the things which has astonished me has been the bitterness of sectaries when the 'auld Kirk' revives. Their sneers at the auld Kirk lose their force, and they find they are flogging, not a dead horse, but a kicking one, and it hurts. I believe no-one need leave the Kirk as long as its foundations remain, however far the generality have departed from it. You can revive the Kirk only from within. But you must observe these points I have tried to make to do so.

Now, I ask nothing of you in response to what I have said, but one thing. Go to God and say, 'O God, take me. That's what You have called me for. Take me, as You took Moody'—and I use his name because I want you to know that I have no prejudice against that wonderful man, but against those who have made his ministry the 'all', the 'be-all and end-all' of the Christian church's task (something he would never have allowed himself). 'Take me, Lord, at whatever cost. Make me a quiet, or roaring flame of fire, as You wish, to burn up the dross of evangelical life in our day, and sear the tails of the demons of ungodliness and filth which are roaming unchecked in society. Then build the church and Kingdom of Jesus Christ. Use me, Lord, use me, for service or sacrifice,

> Just as Thou wilt, and when, and where,
> Until Thy blessed face I see,
> Thy rest, Thy joy, Thy glory share.